STUDY GUIDE
MANAGEMENT ACCOUNTING

Atkinson

Banker

Kaplan

Young

Third Edition

Ella Mae Matsumura *University of Wisconson-Madison*

S. Mark Young *University of Southern California*

Upper Saddle River, New Jersey 07458

Acquisitions editor: Deborah Hoffman
Associate editor: Kathryn Sheehan
Production editor: Carol Zaino
Manufacturer: Phoenix

Copyright ©2001 by Prentice-Hall, Inc., Upper Saddle River, New Jersey, 07458. All rights reserved. Printed in the United States of America. This publication is protected by copyright, and permission should be obtained from the publisher prior to any prohibited reproduction, storage in a retrieval system, or transmission in any form or by any means, electronic, mechanical, photocopying, recording, or likewise. For information regarding permission(s), write to: Rights and Permissions Department.

ISBN 0-13-012542-3

10 9 8 7 6 5 4 3 2 1

Contents

Chapter 1: Management Accounting: Information That Creates Value	1
Chapter 2: The Organization as a System of Activities	17
Chapter 3: Cost Management Concepts and Cost Behavior	31
Chapter 4: Traditional Cost Management Systems	49
Chapter 5: Activity-Based Cost Management Systems	63
Chapter 6: Management Accounting Information for Activity and Process Decisions	81
Chapter 7: Cost Information for Pricing and Product Planning	97
Chapter 8: Capital Budgeting	111
Chapter 9: Management Accounting and Control Systems for Strategic Purposes: Assessing Performance over the Entire Value Chain	127
Chapter 10: Motivating Behavior in Management Accounting and Control Systems	143
Chapter 11: Using Budgets to Achieve Organizational Objectives	163
Chapter 12: Responsibility Centers and Financial Control	181

To the Student

This study guide has been designed to accompany the third edition of Anthony Atkinson, Rajiv Banker, R. S. Kaplan, and S. Mark Young's textbook, *Management Accounting*. The textbook and book of readings are designed to provide students with state-of-the-art material on management accounting. The purpose of the Study Guide is to reinforce what you have learned, and even though it is quite detailed, *it is not a substitute for the textbook*.

For each textbook chapter, there is a corresponding Study Guide chapter that presents the learning objectives, a detailed summary of key terms and concepts, and a comprehensive set of practice test questions and problems. Checkmarked boxes in the Study Guide chapters focus your attention on particular exhibits in the textbook or key points to think about.

The area of management accounting has gained a great deal of importance for managers and employees in all areas. Understanding this topic will help you tremendously in your career, regardless of the path that you take. We hope that you enjoy the textbook and book of readings, and that you find the Study Guide helpful.

Ella Mae Matsumura
School of Business
University of Wisconsin—Madison

S. Mark Young
School of Accounting
University of Southern California

chapter 1

Management Accounting: Information That Creates Value

Learning Objectives

After reading this chapter, you will be able to

1. appreciate the important role that management accounting information plays in manufacturing, service, nonprofit, and governmental organizations

2. discuss the significant differences between management accounting and financial accounting

3. understand how different people in the organization have different demands for management accounting information

4. appreciate how management accounting creates value for organizations and how it relates to operations, marketing, and strategy

5. explain why management accounting information must include both financial and nonfinancial information

6. understand why activities should be the primary focus for measuring and managing performance in organizations

7. appreciate the behavioral and ethical issues faced by management accountants

SUMMARY

This chapter explains how effective design and the use of management accounting information systems can enhance organizational performance. The information produced by these systems is critical to the success of both manufacturing and service organizations in today's globally competitive and technologically challenging environment. The systems must produce accurate, timely, and relevant financial and nonfinancial performance measurements that are crucial to organizational success. An emphasis on the costs incurred and the value created by organizational activities and processes will provide a central focus for management accounting information. The need to customize management accounting information to the particular decision, learning, and control needs of employees and managers is an important theme in this chapter and throughout the book.

REVIEW OF KEY TERMS AND CONCEPTS

> Learning Objective 1: Appreciate the important role that management accounting information plays in manufacturing, service, nonprofit, and governmental organizations.

I. The Role of Management Accounting in Organizations

A. **Management accounting** is the process of planning, designing, measuring and operating nonfinancial and financial information systems that guide management action, motivate behavior, and support and create the cultural values necessary to achieve an organization's strategic, tactical, and operating objectives. More simply, **management accounting** is the process of producing financial and operating information for organizational employees and managers. The process should be driven by the informational needs of individuals *internal* to the organization and should guide their operating and investment decisions.

B. **Management accounting information** includes financial and operating data about an organization's activities, processes, operating units, products, services, and customers.

> Learning Objective 2: Discuss the significant differences between management accounting and financial accounting.

C. In contrast, **financial accounting** differs from management accounting information, as financial accounting information and financial statements are produced for *external* constituencies, such as shareholders, creditors (bankers, bondholders, and suppliers), regulators, and governmental authorities. Because external users rely on the information, the financial statement preparation process is heavily constrained by standard-setting, regulatory, and tax authorities and the auditing requirements of independent accountants.

Textbook **Exhibit 1-1** summarizes and contrasts the basic features of financial and management accounting on the following dimensions: audience, purpose, timeliness, restrictions, type of information, nature of information, and scope. Note how the fundamental difference in primary audience drives differences along the other dimensions.

Learning Objective 3: Understand how different people in the organization have different demands for management accounting information.

Learning Objective 4: Appreciate how management accounting creates value for organizations and how it relates to operations, marketing, and strategy.

Learning Objective 5: Explain why management accounting information must include both financial and nonfinancial information.

II. Diversity of Management Accounting Information: Car Dealership Example

   A. A **mechanic** who repairs and maintains cars performs many activities for which standards have been established for time and quantity of materials. The management accounting system might provide the mechanic with the actual time and quantity of materials used, to help the mechanic assess efficiency. The management accounting system might also report the quality of the mechanic's work, the number and type of repair jobs completed, and cycle time information (elapsed time for a job from start to finish). The information described is operational (nonfinancial) and should be timely. That is, the information might be reported daily or after each job, to be most useful in improving job performance.

   B. The **service department manager** supervises the mechanics and service representatives who interact directly with customers. For the manager's purposes, the management accounting system should provide information on number of mechanic hours spent on repairs and maintenance versus hours available at capacity usage. The manager will also want information on mechanics' efficiency and quality of work, as well as profitability of the service operation or profitability of specific services. She may view profitability reports weekly or monthly. The manager will use information about cost of types of maintenance and repair jobs as input to decisions such as pricing, product mix (repair job promotion), capacity expansion or contraction, and process improvement.

C. The **manager (president) of the dealership** will certainly monitor the dealership's profitability broken down by its major operating departments: new car sales, used car sales, car repairs and service, and parts sales. The president will monitor profitability perhaps weekly or monthly, but will probably not monitor daily operations or profitability on individual jobs.

1. The president will probably desire **benchmarking**, the process of studying and comparing how other best-performing organizations, either internal or external to the firm, perform similar activities and processes.

2. An organization's senior executives monitor **strategic information**, which guides the long-term decision making of the organization. Strategic information can include the profitability of products, services, and customers; competitors' behavior; customer preferences and trends; market opportunities and threats; and technological innovations.

III. Functions of Management Accounting

Textbook **Exhibit 1-2** summarizes the functions of management accounting in the following categories: operational control, product and customer costing, management control, and strategic control. The demand for management accounting information differs at each level of the organization, as described in the car dealership example.

A. **Operational control** is the process of providing feedback to employees and their managers about the efficiency and quality of activities being performed.

B. **Product costing** is the process of measuring and assigning the costs of activities performed to design and produce individual products (and services, for nonmanufacturing companies).

C. **Customer costing** is the process of assigning marketing, selling, distribution, and administrative costs to individual customers so that the cost of serving each customer can be calculated.

D. **Management control** is the process of providing information about the performance of managers and operating units.

E. **Strategic control** is the process of providing information about the organization's long-run competitive performance, market conditions, customer preferences, and technological innovations.

F. Senior executives have begun to monitor a comprehensive, *balanced set of financial and nonfinancial performance indicators* that not only track past performance, but also help provide understanding of drivers of *future* performance. The set of indicators includes information about customers and markets; innovations in products and services; overall quality, process time, and cost of critical internal processes; and capabilities of the organization's employees and systems.

IV. Management Control: Origins in Twentieth-Century Enterprises (Diversified Corporations)

   A. Innovations at DuPont

   1. An **operating budget** is a document that forecasts revenues and expenses during the next operating period, typically a year. The operating budget also authorizes spending on discretionary activities, such as research and development, advertising, maintenance, and employee training.

   2. The **capital budget** is the management document that authorizes spending for resources, such as plant and equipment, that will have multiyear useful lifetimes.

   3. The **return-on-investment formula** is a calculation that relates the profitability of an organizational unit to the investment required to generate that profitability. The formula is often written as the return on sales (the ratio of operating income to sales) multiplied by the ratio of sales to assets employed (or investment). Managers at DuPont used the ROI measure in deciding which divisions should receive additional capital.

   $$ROI = \frac{\text{Operating income}}{\text{Investment}} = \frac{\text{Operating income}}{\text{Sales}} \times \frac{\text{Sales}}{\text{Investment}}$$

   B. Innovations at General Motors

   1. **Decentralized responsibility** allows local division managers to make decisions on pricing, product mix, customer relationships, resource acquisition, materials sourcing, and operating processes without having to seek approval from higher-level managers. Decentralized responsibility also lets local managers use their superior access to information about local opportunities and operating conditions to make better and more timely decisions.

   2. **Centralized control** of operations was accomplished providing senior executives with periodic information about decentralized divisional operations and profitability to assure that division managers were making decisions and taking actions that contribute to overall corporate goals.

   3. The General Motors management accounting system enabled the company to plan, coordinate, control, and evaluate the some-

what independent operating divisions, such as assembly divisions that produced Chevrolet, Pontiac, and Buick automobiles, and component divisions that produced parts.

C. Challenges in the Late Twentieth Century

1. Increased external reporting demands led many organizations to focus on external financial reporting information. Meanwhile, management accounting systems in most organizations stagnated and proved inadequate for the changing and challenging competitive, technological, and market conditions.

2. As an example, American carmakers faced competitive challenges (cost, quality, and cycle time) from European and Japanese carmakers. Obsolete management accounting systems failed to provide accurate and timely information to meet the challenges.

> Learning Objective 1, continued:
> Appreciate the important role that management accounting information plays in manufacturing, service, nonprofit, and governmental organizations.

V. Management Accounting and Control in Service Organizations

Textbook **Exhibit 1-3** provides examples of companies in various service industries. Pick one manufacturing and one service organization with which you are familiar and compare them using points 1 through 3 below.

A. Service Organizations

1. Generally do not produce a product.

2. Have more direct contact with customers, so the organization must be very sensitive to timeliness and quality of service to customers.

3. Now face deregulation and other competitive challenges. Consequently, service organizations, like manufacturing organizations, now require accurate, timely information to improve the quality, timeliness, and efficiency of the activities they perform, as well as to make decisions about their individual products, services, and customers.

B. Government and Nonprofit Organizations

1. Government organizations face pressure for improved performance as citizens demand more responsive and more efficient performance from their local, regional, and national governments. For example, a 1995 Federal Accounting Standards Advisory Board document of "Managerial Cost Accounting and Standards for the Federal Government" stated, "cost information is essential in (1) budgeting and cost control, (2) performance measurement, (3) determining reimbursements and setting fees and prices, (4) program evaluations, and (5) making economic choice decisions."

2. Nonprofit organizations also face pressure for cost and performance measurement (efficiency and effectiveness) from funding governments, foundations, and private individuals.

Learning Objective 6: Understand why activities should be the primary focus for measuring and managing performance in organizations.

VI. Measuring and Managing Activities and Business Processes; Links to Strategy

A. *Measurement of **activities** will be the key organizing principle for studying management accounting information.* **Activities** are the work performed within an organization. An activity brings together people, equipment, materials, energy, and other resources to produce a product or service. Activities should be described using verbs: assemble products, set up machines, respond to customer requests, or design a new service.

B. Cost systems based on activities, called activity-based costing, link organizational spending on resources (people, equipment, materials, and energy) to the products and services produced and delivered to customers. More specifically, activity-based costing (ABC) first assigns resource costs to the activities performed by the organization. Then activity costs are assigned to products, customers, and services that benefit from or are creating the demand for activities.

C. Business processes are series of activities that are linked to perform a specific objective, such as purchasing materials, producing products, maintaining equipment, or servicing customers.

D. Today's management accounting systems must collect and report cost and nonfinancial performance measures, such as process time and quality, for activities and business processes. Such measurements emphasize *total cost reduction* and *process improvement*, not just improving efficiencies for individual workers, machines, and departments, which was traditionally the focus of management accounting information.

E. A focus on business processes enables companies to link their management accounting systems to the organization's strategy. The management accounting systems are vital for communicating the strategy of the business and for aligning all organizational activities and processes to help implement the strategy. Strategy types include *operational excellence* (McDonald's), *product leadership* (Intel), or *great customer service* (Home Depot).

Learning Objective 7: Appreciate the behavioral and ethical issues faced by management accountants.

VII. Behavioral and Ethical Issues Faced by Management Accountants

A. The design and introduction of new measurements and systems must be accompanied by an analysis of the behavioral and organizational reactions to the measurements. Managers and employees may take unexpected and undesirable actions to influence their score on performance measures or may resist the new system.

B. Organizational leadership plays a critical role in fostering a culture of high ethical standards. Beyond the example set by senior executives, companies can use control systems to foster high ethical standards among their employees.

1. A **beliefs system** is the explicit set of statements that senior managers communicate formally and reinforce systematically to provide basic values, purpose, and direction for the organization. Beliefs systems inspire people to higher values and missions but do not communicate what behaviors and actions are unacceptable.

Textbook **Exhibit 1-4** displays Johnson & Johnson's credo. How do the company's executives communicate the credo to employees? What role did the credo play when the company faced a crisis with contaminated Tylenol pills?

2. **Boundary systems** communicate what actions must never be taken, such as violating clients' privacy. Boundary systems delineate the acceptable domain of activity for organizational participants and describe the limits on individuals' opportunity-seeking behavior.

Textbook **Exhibit 1-5** provides an excerpt from the standards of ethical conduct for management accountants. Contrast Exhibit 1-4 (Johnson & Johnson's credo) with this exhibit, which includes several statements on prohibited actions.

PRACTICE TEST QUESTIONS AND PROBLEMS

True/False

_____ 1. Management accounting information includes the cost and profitability of an organization's products, departments, services, and activities.

_____ 2. Management accounting information is generated primarily for use by constituencies external to the firm.

_____ 3. Management accounting information is regulated by government authorities.

_____ 4. Management accounting information encompasses operational and nonfinancial information.

_____ 5. Companies have considerable choice in the design of their management accounting systems.

_____ 6. Many of today's service and manufacturing organizations demand different and better management accounting information than in the early twentieth century.

_____ 7. Government and nonprofit organizations have little use for management accounting information.

_____ 8. Functions are the key organizing principle for studying management accounting information.

_____ 9. There is little an organization can do to foster high ethical standards among the organization's managers and employees.

_____ 10. The demand for management accounting information differs depending on the level of the organization.

Multiple-Choice

1. Management accounting information is developed for the following users, EXCEPT
   (a) shareholders.
   (b) middle managers.
   (c) senior executives.
   (d) operators/workers.

2. Which of the following roles does management accounting information NOT serve?
   (a) Operational control
   (b) Strategic control
   (c) Management control
   (d) External control

3. Which of the following is the president of an automobile dealership LEAST likely to monitor?
   (a) Profit and loss on individual repair jobs
   (b) Weekly financial reports on the dealership's profitability
   (c) Monthly financial reports on profitability of major operating departments
   (d) Customer satisfaction indexes

4. If operating income is $15,000, sales are $120,000, and investment is $300,000, return on investment is
   (a) 12.5%.
   (b) 5.0%.
   (c) 40.0%.
   (d) 250.0%.

5. At the heart of the senior executives' comprehensive, balanced set of financial and nonfinancial performance indicators linked to the organization's strategy is a focus on
   (a) business processes.
   (b) checking that debits equal credits.
   (c) improving efficiencies for individual workers.
   (d) neutrality of the management accounting information.

6. Customer costing is useful for determining
   (a) the product cost that a customer expects.
   (b) the product price that a customer expects.
   (c) the cost of serving each customer.
   (d) the total cost that a customer is willing to pay for products.

7. Historically, service companies have used management accounting information
   (a) more intensively than manufacturing companies.
   (b) less intensively than manufacturing companies.
   (c) with the same intensity as manufacturing companies.
   (d) only for product costing.

8. The first step in using activity-based costing is to
   (a) assign activities to products.
   (b) assign resources to products.
   (c) assign resource costs to activities.
   (d) assign resource costs to products.

Completion

1. Management accounting information includes financial measurements plus operational and physical measurements on _____, _____, _____, _____, and _____.

2. The design and introduction of new measurements and systems must anticipate _____ and _____ reactions to the measurements.

3. In contrast to traditional management accounting information that was collected and reported for individual departments, current management accounting systems must measure cost and nonfinancial performance measures for _____ and _____ _____.

4. Studying how other best-performing organizations, either internal or external to the firm, perform similar activities or processes, is called _____.

5. Management accounting serves several functions: operational control, product and customer costing, _____ control, _____ control, and _____ control.

6. _____ _____ refers to the authority that local division managers have to make decisions on pricing and product mix based on their superior access to local information.

7. Business strategy types include _____ _____ (for example, McDonald's), _____ _____ (for example, Intel), or _____ _____ _____ (for example, Home Depot).

8. The measurement of _____, which can be viewed as the mechanism by which organizational resources and employees accomplish work, will be the key organizing principle for studying management accounting information.

9. Business _____ are collections of activities for accomplishing organizational objectives.

10. Recently, senior executives have begun to monitor a balanced set of performance indicators that includes a variety of nonfinancial information, particularly information about _____ and _____, innovations in _____ and _____, overall quality, process time, and cost of _____ _____, and capabilities of the organization's _____ and _____.

Problems

1. Assume that you are designing a management accounting system for an express mail delivery service. Determine the management accounting information needs for each of the following employees:

    (a) delivery people

    (b) local manager

    (c) regional manager

2. Contrast manufacturing and service organizations and how their management accounting information needs might differ.

SOLUTIONS TO PRACTICE TEST QUESTIONS AND PROBLEMS

True/False

1. True. Management accounting information encompasses all of these functions as it produces information that helps workers, managers, and executives make better decisions and improve processes and performance.

2. False. Management accounting information is generated for use primarily by constituencies internal to the firm.

3. False. Management accounting is not regulated by the government. Recall that management accounting information is generated primarily for use by individuals within an organization.

4. True. Management accounting information encompasses not only operational and nonfinancial information, such as quality and process times, but also measures of customer satisfaction and new product performance.

5. True. Managers should design systems that provide information useful for an organization's managers and employees. The need to customize management accounting information to the particular decision, learning, and control needs of employees and managers is an important theme throughout the book.

6. True. During the last quarter of the twentieth century, both manufacturing and service organizations discovered a need for improved management accounting information as they faced increasingly challenging competitive environments.

7. False. Government organizations face increasing pressure for improved performance as citizens demand more responsive and more efficient performance from various levels of government.

8. False. Measurement of *activities* is the key organizing principle for studying management accounting information.

9. False. Organizational leadership plays a critical role in fostering a culture of high ethical standards. Beyond the example set by senior executives, companies can use control systems called *beliefs systems* and *boundary systems* to foster high ethical standards among their employees.

10. True. Demands for management accounting information will differ depending on the level of the organization, such as the operator level, the middle management level, and the top executive level.

Multiple-Choice

1. a. Management accounting information is developed for internal users such as middle managers, senior executives, and operators/workers, rather than for external users such as shareholders.

2. d. Management accounting information is used for (a) operational control, which is the process of providing feedback to employees and their managers about the efficiency of activities being performed; (b) strategic control, which is the process of providing information about the competitive performance of the overall business unit, both financially and in meeting customers' expectations; and (c) management control, which is the process of providing information about the performance of managers and operating units.

3. a. The president is likely to monitor higher-level performance measures, as in responses (b), (c), and (d). The service department manager will likely monitor profit and loss on individual repair jobs.

4. b. ROI is equal to Operating Income/Investment. Therefore,
ROI = $15,000/$300,000 = 5%.
ROI can also be written as
(Operating Income/Sales) × (Sales/Investment) = ($15,000/$120,000)
× ($120,000/$300,000) = (12.5%)(40%) = 5%.

5. a. A focus on business processes enables companies to link their management accounting systems to the organization's strategy. The balanced set of performance indicators can help organizations communicate the business strategy and align all organizational activities and processes to help implement the strategy. Responses (b) and (c) are incorrect because they are not the primary focus of the balanced set of performance measures linked to strategy. Response (d) is incorrect because management accounting information is not neutral, but rather influences people's behavior.

6. c. Customer costing is useful for determining the cost of serving each customer. Customer costing can include assignments of marketing, selling, distribution, and administrative costs to individual customers.

7. b. Historically, service companies have used management accounting information less intensively than manufacturing companies. Now, however, service companies face deregulation and other competitive challenges. Consequently, service organizations, like manufacturing organizations, now require accurate,

timely information to improve the quality, timeliness, and efficiency of the activities they perform, as well as to make decision about their individual products, services, and customers.

8. c. The first step in using activity-based costing is to assign resource costs to activities. Then activity costs are assigned to products, customers, and services that benefit from or are creating the demand for activities.

Completion

1. processes, technologies, suppliers, customers, competitors

2. behavioral, organizational

3. activities, business processes

4. benchmarking

5. operational, management, strategic

6. Decentralized responsibility

7. operational excellence, product leadership, great customer service

8. activities

9. processes

10. customers and markets, products and services, critical internal processes, employees and systems

Problems

1. Although no one correct response to this question exists, some possible answers follow.

    (a) Delivery people will probably want to know what the standards of work performance are on several dimensions so that they have a gauge on what is expected at work. They also need feedback information about their average delivery time per package, resources used (such as fuel), amount of breakage of package contents, etc.

    (b) The local manager will want summary information about each delivery person on such dimensions as on-time delivery, number of errors, breakage, resources spent per driver, customer satisfaction, number of speeding/parking tickets, and number of deliveries made. These measures will probably be recorded on a daily or weekly basis and compared to work standards that have been established.

(c) The regional manager will want to see weekly or monthly summaries of all of the delivery stations in his or her area. The summaries will include the average cost per delivery, volume of packages delivered, amount of breakage, number of customer complaints, and overall profitability of delivery stations.

2. Manufacturing companies produce products, whereas service companies generally do not produce anything that can be inventoried. Service firms rely a great deal on human interaction. For instance, dealing with a bank teller or buying insurance from an insurance agent are examples where human interaction is important. In contrast, a person who buys an automobile owns a tangible product that can be evaluated by how the car handles, what it looks like, the quality of the components, etc. Quality can be assessed and controlled for products more easily than for services. Often a defect can be corrected on an assembly line, but an uncomfortable ride or a rude flight attendant can be difficult or impossible to control in advance. Thus, services are subject to much more direct customer satisfaction and dissatisfaction than is manufacturing.

chapter 2

The Organization as a System of Activities

*L*earning *O*bjectives

After reading this chapter, you will be able to

1. understand how organizations define objectives and use these objectives to define operating priorities

2. think of the organization as a sequence of activities in a value chain

3. demonstrate how performance measures help organization members manage the value chain

4. describe the process that organizations use to reduce costs by focusing on activity performance

SUMMARY

The perspective that the organization is a sequence of activities in a value chain forms the foundation for the remainder of this book. This sequence of activities should be evaluated from the customers' perspectives on service, quality, and cost. Organization members can continuously improve the value, quality, and cost performance of activities by charting the organization's process activities and identifying activities whose costs exceed the value they add to the product. Management accounting, described as "information that creates value" in Chapter 1, provides information about cost and other process details to help organization members manage the value chain.

REVIEW OF KEY TERMS AND CONCEPTS

> Learning Objective 1: Understand how organizations define objectives and use these objectives to define operating priorities.

I. The Nature of the Organization's Objectives

　　A. **Strategy** is the process of choosing target customers and deciding how to serve those customers.

　　B. Given decisions on how the organization will meet its customers' or beneficiaries' requirements, decision makers design the operating systems or sequence of activities to meet those requirements, as well as performance measurement systems (including costs).

 Textbook **Exhibit 2-1** summarizes the strategic planning perspective, beginning with the choice of the target set of customers. The target customers' requirements translate into the organization's objectives. Processes (sequences of activities) are designed to meet the objectives, and performance in meeting the objectives is monitored and assessed. Corporate strategy coordinates the needs of the organization's stakeholders (suppliers and other partners, employees, customers, owners or principals, and the broader community) into a cohesive plan.

II. Three Levels of Strategy

　　A. **Organizational-level strategy making** is the process of choosing what business the organization is in. (For example, Wal-Mart is a mass merchandiser. Other companies have a specific narrow product focus.)

　　B. **Business-level strategy making** is the process of choosing the organization's target customers and the broad approach necessary to meet its needs. (For example, a gasoline company might target customers who are less interested in low cost than in service, credit card privileges, and a convenience store.) **Value proposition** refers to a clear and short statement of competitive value that the organization will deliver to its target customers—how it will compete for or satisfy its customers. (Wal-Mart, for example, offers low cost and wide selection.)

　　C. **Operational-level (tactical-level) strategy making** reflects the way the organization pursues its business-level strategy. An effective operational-level strategy must deliver the organization's value proposition, and it must reflect the organization's strengths. (For example, Wal-Mart's operational-level strategy supports its strategy of large selection at low cost.)

Textbook **Exhibit 2-2** summarizes responses on spending of application dollars, from a recent study of the 100 top innovators in manufacturing. The strategy of these firms is to invest heavily in ERP and related applications as springboards to e-business.

Learning Objective 2: Think of the organization as a sequence of activities in a value chain.

III. The Organization as a Sequence of Activities or a Value Chain

   A. Organizations perform a sequence of *activities* that provide goods or services, called *products*, to their *customers*.

   B. A **value chain** is a sequence of activities whose objective is to provide a product to a customer or to provide an intermediate good or service in a larger value chain. *Each step in the value chain should contribute more to the ultimate value of the product than its cost.*

   C. An **activity** is a unit of work, or task, with a specific goal. Examples of activities are processing an insurance claim, waiting on a customer in a restaurant, and welding two components together. Because activities create costs, understanding the nature of reasons and for activities is important in reducing costs. There are four broad categories of activities in the value chain:

      1. **Customer management activities:** Understanding customer requirements.

      2. **Innovation activities:** Developing products that meet customer requirements.

      3. **Operations activities:** Designing systems to handle inbound logistics; managing suppliers, operations and manufacturing; and managing the flow of products to customers.

      4. **Service activities:** Providing customers with after-sales service.

 Textbook **Exhibit 2-3** diagrams the four categories of activities listed above.

Learning Objective 3: Demonstrate how performance measures help organization members manage the value chain.

IV. Focusing the Value Chain

   A. The organization's target customers define its key success factors, which can be grouped in the following categories:

   1. **Quality** refers to how well the product's operating characteristics conform to what the organization promises customers.

   2. **Service** consists of the product's tangible and intangible features provided to the customer; service is also known as value in use.

   3. **Price** refers to the lifetime cost of the product to the customer and includes purchase price, operating costs, maintenance costs, and disposition costs.

Textbook **Exhibit 2-4** illustrates elements of the relationship between service and quality. Note that the *service gap* is the difference between what the customer wants and what the customer is promised; the *quality gap* is the difference between what the customer is promised and what the customer is given.

   B. **Organization control** is the activity of assessing the value chain's performance from the perspective of the organization's objectives. Note that an effective planning and control system should factor in the objectives and strategies of the organization. Organization control includes four components:

   1. Specifying objectives (plan)
   2. Communicating objectives to organization members (communicate and implement)
   3. Monitoring performance relating to objectives (measure)
   4. Acting on discrepancies between actual and target performance (revise)

   C. **Process control**, or **operations control**, is the activity of assessing the operating performance of each unit in the value chain in meeting customer requirements. Process control compares short-term performance to short-run targets or standards and focuses on directing, evaluating, and improving the processes the organization uses to deliver goods and services to its customers.

V. Performance Measurement, Management Accounting, and Operations Control

   A. **Performance measurement** is the activity of measuring the performance of an activity, manager, organizational unit, or value chain. An effective system of operations performance measurement includes critical performance indicators that:

1. Consider each activity and the organization from the **customer's perspective.**

2. Evaluate each activity using **customer-validated performance measures**—tools used to reflect customer requirements and help employees manage and improve the value chain's processes and activities in order to please customers.

   a. An **input** is what the organization puts into a process, such as employee time, production cost, or capacity used.

   b. An **output** is a physical measure of production or activity, such as the number of units produced or the amount of time spent being productive.

   c. An **outcome** is the *value* the customer attributes to the result of an activity, such as the number of good units of production and the amount of client satisfaction generated by a service.

   d. Because outcomes are an assessment of customer value, they provide a better measure than inputs or outputs of what the relevant process is contributing to the organization.

Textbook **Exhibit 2-5** provides examples of inputs, outputs, and outcomes for various organizations. Note that outcomes can be more difficult to measure than inputs and outputs.

3. Are **comprehensive** in considering all facets of activity performance that affect customers. If a performance measurement system does not assess all facets of relevant performance, a decision maker may trade off relevant but unmeasured facets of performance for those that are measured. Examples include Domino's Pizza's focus on delivery speed and Harley-Davidson's focus on reduced manufacturing and delivery time.

4. Provide **feedback** to organizational employees on how to identify problems and improve. An effective performance measurement program provides understandable feedback measures that will help people who manage the value chain to identify problems and suggest solutions.

B. Performance Measures as Aids in Operations Control

1. Control may be exercised by developing standard procedures and ensuring compliance with the procedures. Information is

used to motivate people to follow procedures and to verify that they follow them. **Task control** refers to systems or procedures designed to ensure that employees follow stated procedures or rules. For example, a fast-food restaurant provides standardized rules for preparing and serving items.

2. Control may also be exercised by hiring qualified people who understand the organization's objectives and giving them the authority to make decisions to help the organization achieve its objectives. Information is provided to these people to facilitate their decision making. **Results control** refers to a system focused on results or outcomes that is designed to motivate decision-making behavior to achieve the organization's behavior. For example, a store manager might be instructed to design an advertising campaign to enhance the company's reputation.

C. Performance Targets

1. Realized, or actual, performance may be compared with a target performance level. A performance *variance*, which is a discrepancy between the actual and planned performance levels, signals a potential problem for investigation and correction.

2. Process performance targets may be based on *estimated potential*, such as engineering standards.

3. Performance targets may be based on *improving past performance*. **Continuous improvement** involves continuously making incremental changes to improve the processes that the organization performs to meet its customers' requirements.

4. Targets based on potential or past performance do not reflect what competitors are doing. To counteract this shortcoming, organizations may use **benchmarking**, the process of studying and comparing how other organizations perform similar activities and processes, then adapting the best practices of other organizations to improve the firm's own performance. The other organizations can be internal or external to the firm (even in a different industry) and are selected because they are known to have excellent performance for the benchmarked process.

5. Targets may be chosen to meet or exceed customer expectations.

Learning Objective 4: Describe the process that organizations use to reduce costs by focusing on activity performance.

VI. Cost as a Process Performance Measure

   A. **Managing by the numbers** is an approach to cost cutting that focuses on reducing the budget, or cost allowance, allowed for a particular activity. Managing by the numbers has the following three problems:

      1. It is ineffective because it focuses on getting employees to work faster, longer, or harder, which may lead to poor quality, poor service, and unhappy employees.

      2. It assumes that cost is the only relevant measure of an activity's performance.

      3. It does not recognize the reasons that costs exist.

   B. Life-cycle costing embodies a broader vision of how costs can be used and how the type of cost information needed will vary across decision-making contexts. **Life-cycle costing** is a systematic consideration of product costs during the product's lifetime; these costs include costs of development, introduction, production, distribution, after-sales service, takeback (recovering postconsumer waste), and product abandonment.

   C. Effective cost control involves understanding how customer requirements create the need for activities, how activities create costs, and what activities are efficient and effective.

      1. An organization may manage by using activity data rather than cost data because activity data not only help identify problems, but may also suggest how to solve the problems. For example, compiling a list of defects may allow the organization to identify problem areas that result in defects. Activity information can serve as *diagnostic information to improve performance*. **Variances**, which are the differences between planned and actual costs, signal excessive costs but do not suggest the causes.

      2. Activity *costs* can help to set priorities for process improvement.

      3. Accounting systems track costs created by some underlying activity, whether it is resource use or resource acquisition.

      4. Organizations can reduce costs by eliminating the need for activities or by improving the performance of existing activities.

      5. **Reengineering** involves evaluating the process objectives and redesigning the entire process to make it less costly.

      6. An **efficient activity** consumes no excess resources. An **inefficient activity** requires more resources than necessary to produce the desired outcome. Many organizations continuously study their processes to discover better ways of doing them.

D. **Activity analysis (value analysis** or **activity-based management)** is an approach to operations control that involves applying the steps of continuous improvement to an activity. Five steps are involved:

1. **Identify** the process objectives, defined by what the organization's target customers want or expect from the process.

2. **Chart,** by recording from start to finish, the activities used to complete a product or service.

3. **Classify** activities by comparing their cost with the value they add to the product from the customer's perspective.

4. **Continuously improve** the efficiency of all activities. Benchmarking may support continuous improvement.

5. **When possible, eliminate activities** whose costs exceed their value by reengineering or redesigning existing processes.

PRACTICE TEST QUESTIONS AND PROBLEMS

True/False

_____ 1. Strategy is the process of choosing target customers and deciding how to serve those customers.

_____ 2. Organizational-level strategy making reflects the way the organization pursues its business-level strategy.

_____ 3. Stakeholders to the organization include employees, partners, and the community.

_____ 4. Each step in a value chain should contribute something more to the ultimate value of the product than its cost.

_____ 5. *Effectiveness* means using the fewest possible resources to meet stated objectives.

_____ 6. Quality is usually defined in the abstract, independent of a service or product.

_____ 7. Outputs and outcomes are identical.

_____ 8. One of the problems in "managing by the numbers" is that it simply takes too long.

_____ 9. Targets based on engineering standards or improving past performance are the best performance targets.

_____ 10. Input measurement does not focus on effectiveness in meeting customer requirements.

Multiple-Choice

1. Each of the following is a part of the strategic planning perspective, EXCEPT
    (a) choosing the target set of customers.
    (b) designing processes to meet the organization's objectives.
    (c) monitoring and assessing performance in meeting the organization's objectives.
    (d) managing by the numbers.

2. An organization is efficient if
    (a) it achieves its objectives.
    (b) it uses the fewest resources possible to achieve its objectives.
    (c) it uses the largest amount of resources possible to achieve its objectives.
    (d) total planned output is achieved regardless of inputs used.

3. Business-level strategy making
    (a) is the process of choosing what business an organization is in.
    (b) reflects the way an organization delivers its value proposition.
    (c) is the process of choosing the organization's target customers and the broad approach necessary to meet its needs.
    (d) refers to a clear and short statement of competitive value that an organization will deliver to its target customers.

4. Which of the four broad categories of activities in the value chain pertains to managing the flow of products to customers?
    (a) Customer management activities
    (b) Innovation activities
    (c) Operations activities
    (d) Service activities

5. An effective performance measurement system contains critical performance indicators that do each of the following, EXCEPT
    (a) consider each activity and the organization itself from the customer's perspective.
    (b) evaluate each activity using customer-validated measures.
    (c) provide feedback to help identify problems.
    (d) consider each activity and the organization itself only from an internal management perspective.

6. Organization control is
    (a) the relentless search to find ways to improve the organization.
    (b) applicable only in manufacturing organizations.
    (c) the set of methods and tools that organization members use to keep the organization on track toward achieving its objectives.
    (d) an organization's search for the best way to do something as practiced by another organization.

7. Continuous improvement involves all of the following, EXCEPT
    (a) understanding the activities that the organization undertakes to meet its customers' requirements.
    (b) improving the performance of value-added activities.
    (c) redesigning entire processes.
    (d) eliminating inefficient activities.

8. Process control involves all of the following, EXCEPT
    (a) comparing short-term performance to appropriate standards.
    (b) evaluating the organization's processes.
    (c) improving the organization's processes.
    (d) assessing a value chain's performance from the organization's perspective.

9. Which of the following is NOT true?
    (a) Quality is defined as conformance to specifications.
    (b) In evaluating price as a key success factor relevant to target customers, an organization considers only the customers' purchase price.
    (c) The service gap is the difference between what the customer wants and what the customer is promised.
    (d) The quality gap is the difference between what the customer is promised and what the customer is given.

10. An approach to operations control that involves applying the steps of continuous improvement to an activity is referred to by all of the following, EXCEPT
    (a) reengineering.
    (b) value analysis.
    (c) activity analysis.
    (d) activity-based management.

Completion

1. Most organizations have five groups of stakeholders: the employees, _____, _____, _____, and _____.

2. An activity is a unit of _____ with a specific _____.

3. Organizations perform a sequence of _____ that provide goods or services to their customers.

4. A _____ _____ is a sequence of activities whose objective is to provide a product to a customer or to provide an intermediate good or service in a larger _____ _____.

5. Key success factors related to the ability of an organization to meet customer requirements can be grouped into the following categories: _____, _____, and _____.

6. Service refers to the product's _____ _____, such as performance and taste, and its _____ _____, such as how people are treated when making the purchase decision.

7. Quality is the difference between the _____ and _____ level of service.

8. An _____ is how the customer values the result of an activity.

9. _____ _____ refers to systems or procedures designed to ensure that employees follow stated procedures or rules.

10. _____ is the process of studying and comparing how other organizations perform similar activities and processes.

Problems

1. What are key success factors for a major airline?

2. List as many inefficient activities involved in a manufacturing facility as you can. Can all of these be eliminated, and, if so, how?

SOLUTIONS TO PRACTICE TEST QUESTIONS AND PROBLEMS

True/False

1. True. Strategy is the process of choosing target customers and deciding how to serve those customers. The target customers' requirements translate into the organization's objectives. Processes are then designed to meet the objectives. Corporate strategy coordinates the needs of the organization's stakeholders into a cohesive plan.

2. False. *Operational-level (tactical-level)* strategy making reflects the way the organization pursues its business-level strategy.

3. True. All are organizational stakeholders. Customers and owners are also stakeholders.

4. True. Each step in a value chain should contribute something more to the ultimate value of the product than its cost.

5. False. This is the definition of efficiency.

6. False. Quality is defined relative to the product or service.

7. False. Outputs are a physical measure of activity, whereas outcomes are the values attributed to the output by the customer.

8. False. There are three problems, but length of time is not one of them. Managing by the numbers is ineffective, assumes that cost is the only relevant measure of an activity's performance, and does not recognize the reasons that costs exist.

9. False. Targets based on engineering standards (potential performance) or improving past performance do not reflect what competitors are doing. An organization may choose instead to benchmark against other internal or external organizations, or may set targets to meet or exceed customer expectations.

10. True. An input is what the organization puts into a process. *Outcome* focuses on value the customer attributes to the result of an activity.

Multiple-Choice

1. d. Managing by the numbers is an approach to cost cutting that focuses on reducing the budget, or cost allowance. Managing by the numbers is ineffective, assumes that cost is the only relevant measure of an activity's performance, and does not recognize the reasons that costs exist.

2. b. An organization is efficient if it uses the fewest resources possible to achieve its objectives.

3. c. Response (a) refers to *organizational-level* strategy making and response (b) relates to *operational-level* strategy making. Response (d) defines *value proposition*.

4. c. Managing the flow of products to customers is part of operations activities, which also include designing systems to handle inbound logistics, and managing suppliers, operations, and manufacturing.

5. d. The key is the customer's perspective, not internal management's.

6. c. Organization control consists of a set of tools and methods to keep the organization on track.

7. c. Continuous improvement treats existing processes as given and tries to make them less costly; response (c) describes reengineering, which involves evaluating process objectives and redesigning entire processes.

8. d. Process control involves all of the responses except (d), which refers to organization control.

9. b. In evaluating price as a key success factor relevant to target customers, an organization considers the lifetime cost of the product to the customer. Consequently, price includes purchase price, operating costs, maintenance costs, and disposition costs.

10. a. Reengineering involves evaluating process objectives and redesigning entire processes.

Completion

1. partners, owners/principals, community, customers

2. work, goal

3. activities

4. value chain, value chain

5. service, quality, price

6. tangible features, intangible features

7. promised, realized

8. outcome

9. Task control

10. Benchmarking

Problems

1. Key success factors for a major airline are:

    (a) Providing safe planes. Planes must be maintained and inspected carefully on a regular basis and no defects tolerated.

    (b) Price of tickets. Ticket prices are critical given the level of competition.

    (c) On-time departure and arrival. This means that the ticket collection and seating procedures must be efficient, and the plane must be fueled, serviced, and inspected, and baggage loaded promptly.

(d) Passenger comfort and service. Seating should be comfortable, meals good (or at least edible!), flight attendants courteous, and flight attendants must also be able to deal with difficult passengers and other problems that arise.

(e) Excellent performance on all of these factors will lead to the most critical variable of all, which is **repeat business**.

2. The broad categories of inefficient activities typically include moving raw materials and work-in-process, storing these items, and inspecting them. Each of these three activities does not really add anything to the product that the customer values. However, each activity may be necessary, depending on the way the production facility is designed. One way to reduce or eliminate all of these activities is to employ a manufacturing philosophy such as just-in-time (JIT). Under this philosophy, raw materials are delivered by outside vendors, just as they are needed. Work-in-process is eliminated because the JIT system allows only one unit to be worked on at a time. Further, under JIT, because each employee is responsible for quality, there is no need for a separate inspection department of personnel. If it is not possible to use a full-blown JIT system, some aspects of the philosophy can be employed.

chapter 3

Cost Management Concepts and Cost Behavior

After reading this chapter, you will be able to

1. explain why the appropriate derivation of a cost depends on how the cost will be used
2. explain why management accountants have developed the notions of long-run and short-run costs and how these different costs are used in decision making
3. state the difference between flexible costs and capacity-related costs and why the difference is important
4. show why the concept of opportunity cost is used in short-run decision making and how opportunity cost relates to conventional accounting costs
5. explain the notion of life-cycle cost and how that idea is used in new product and product purchasing decisions

SUMMARY

This chapter's theme is "different costs for different purposes." Preparers of external financial statements distinguish manufacturing and nonmanufacturing costs in developing cost of goods sold for the income statement and inventory valuation for the balance sheet. Costs for internal planning and evaluation purposes are developed in accordance with the intended use, subject to a cost-benefit trade-off that considers the cost of producing the desired information. Useful contrasts in cost classifications include direct versus indirect with respect to a cost object, short run versus long run, and flexible versus capacity related. The concept of opportunity cost provides insights in short-run decision making. Modern thinking about cost behavior uses a hierarchy of activity levels: unit level, batch level, product sustaining, customer sustaining, and business sustaining. The chapter concludes by discussing life-cycle costing and its importance in managing products.

REVIEW OF KEY TERMS AND CONCEPTS

> Learning Objective 1: Explain why the appropriate derivation of a cost depends on how the cost will be used.

I. Different Costs for Different Purposes

    A. Cost Terms for Computing the Cost of Something

        1. A **cost object** is something for which a cost must be computed. Examples include a product, a product line, or a department.

        2. A **direct cost** is a cost of a resource or activity that is acquired for or used by a single cost object. The cloth for one shirt is a direct cost for the shirt.

        3. An **indirect cost** is a cost of a resource that was acquired to be used by more than one cost object. The cost of a sewing machine to make various items of clothing is an indirect cost for each piece of clothing.

 Textbook **Exhibit 3-1** illustrates how distortions in costing cost objects called product lines can arise when indirect costs are inappropriately or inaccurately allocated.

> Learning Objective 3: State the difference between flexible costs and capacity-related costs and why the difference is important.

    B. Organizing Costs Based on the Way They Are Created

        1. **Flexible resources** are resources whose costs are proportional to the amount of the resource used. That is, the costs vary with production activity. These resources are acquired as needed. Electric power to operate sewing machines is an example of a flexible resource.

        2. The costs of flexible resources are called **flexible costs**. Flexible costs are always direct costs, but are sometimes treated as indirect costs if it is inconvenient to account for them as direct costs and the cost is only a small part of total costs. For example, the cost of thread in a shirt might be treated as an indirect cost even though it is a flexible cost.

3. **Capacity-related resources** are acquired and paid for in advance of when the work is done.

4. The costs associated with capacity-related resources are called **capacity-related costs**. Depreciation on buildings is an example of a capacity-related cost.

5. Labor costs were originally flexible costs. Because scheduling and union considerations guarantee wages to be paid in the short run regardless if work is available, most organizations now treat labor costs as capacity related rather than flexible.

> Learning Objective 1, continued:
> Explain why the appropriate derivation of a cost depends on how the cost will be used.

II. Using Cost Information Outside the Organization

A. **Generally accepted accounting principles (GAAP)** prescribe how costs are to be determined for external reporting. GAAP focuses on process rather than the decision relevance of the resulting cost allocations. The intended result is costs that are computed consistently through time and across different organizations. When developing costs for external financial statements, accounting systems usually classify costs by type (product and period) and function (manufacturing and nonmanufacturing).

B. Costs versus Expenses

1. **Cost** is the monetary value of goods and services expended to obtain current or future benefits.

2. **Expenses** are costs of goods or services that have expired, that is, have been used up in the process of creating goods and services. For example, the cost of a product sold becomes cost of goods expense on the income statement. The cost of unsold goods appears as an asset in the balance sheet.

C. Classifying Costs by Type: Product versus Period Costs

1. **Product costs** are costs associated with the manufacture of products.

2. **Period costs** are costs treated as expenses in the period in which they are incurred because they cannot be associated with the manufacture of products. Examples include administrative, marketing, research and development, and selling costs.

D. Classifying Costs by Function: Manufacturing versus Nonmanufacturing Costs

   1. **Manufacturing costs** are all costs of transforming raw materials into finished products. These costs include flexible costs related to material and labor and capacity-related costs. Manufacturing costs are classified as direct and indirect costs.

      a. **Direct manufacturing costs** are those that can be traced easily to the product manufactured or service rendered. **Direct materials cost** is the cost of all materials and parts that can be traced directly to the product. **Direct labor cost** is the cost of labor paid based on the amount of work done.

      b. **Indirect manufacturing costs** are all manufacturing costs other than direct manufacturing costs. The process of assigning indirect manufacturing costs to products involves allocating a fair share of the indirect cost to the products. Indirect manufacturing costs include equipment and wages and benefits paid to production supervisors.

   2. **Nonmanufacturing costs** are all costs other than manufacturing costs. Traditionally, these costs are considered period costs and are expenses in the period in which they are incurred. These include:

      a. **Distribution costs**, which involve delivering finished products to customers.

      b. **Selling costs**, which include sales personnel salaries and commissions and other sales office expenses.

      c. **Marketing costs**, which include advertising and promotion expenses.

      d. **After-sales costs**, which involve dealing with customers after the sale and include warranty repairs and the cost of maintaining help and complaint lines.

      e. **Research and development costs**, which include expenditures for designing and bringing new products to market.

      f. **General and administrative costs**, which include expenses such as the CEO's salary, legal and general accounting costs, and those costs that do not come under any of the other categories listed.

Textbook **Exhibit 3-2** summarizes the relationship between product and period costs and manufacturing and nonmanufacturing costs. Note the contrasting pairs of concepts, especially between the functions of manufacturing and nonmanufacturing and how they relate to inventory valuation and determination of cost of goods sold for external financial reporting.

Also note that both manufacturing and nonmanufacturing costs can be flexible or capacity related and direct or indirect.

III. Using Cost Information Inside the Organization

    A. Costs serve many different purposes within an organization. The purposes can be classified into two broad categories: *planning* and *evaluation*. Planning includes budgeting and decision making. Evaluation includes profitability analysis and control of process efficiency and effectiveness.

    B. *Cost-benefit trade-off:* In developing cost information for internal purposes, the benefit of developing cost information should outweigh the cost of developing the costs.

    C. *Different costs for different purposes:* The nature of a decision defines the nature of the required cost, the way it should be computed, and the value of any cost number. A cost number that is useful for one decision may be useless for another decision.

> Learning Objective 4: Show why the concept of opportunity cost is used in short-run decision making and how opportunity cost relates to conventional accounting costs.

    D. An **opportunity cost** is the sacrifice incurred when using resources for one purpose instead of another. The opportunity cost of a resource is zero if there is excess capacity of that resource. Opportunity costs are implicit costs because they do not appear anywhere in the accounting records.

> Learning Objective 3, continued:
> State the difference between flexible costs and capacity related costs and why the difference is important.

IV. Comparing Cost Classification Systems

Textbook **Exhibit 3-3** summarizes the distinctions between direct and indirect costs and between flexible and capacity-related costs. Recall that costs are classified as direct or indirect with respect to a specified cost object. This rule is helpful: *Direct* means that the resource that created the cost was acquired for, and used by, a single cost object.

A. All flexible costs are direct costs because they vary directly with use. However, flexible costs are sometimes treated as indirect costs if it is inconvenient to account for them as direct costs and if the cost is only a small part of total costs. For example, the cost of glue in a large bookshelf might be treated as an indirect cost even though it is a flexible cost.

B. Capacity-related costs can be direct or indirect.

Learning Objective 2: Explain why management accountants have developed the notions of long-run and short-run costs and how these different costs are used in decision making.

V. Long-Run and Short-Run Costs

A. *Short run* is the period over which a decision maker cannot adjust capacity. The only costs that vary in the short run are flexible costs, which vary in proportion to production.

B. *Long-run* costs are the sum of flexible and capacity-related costs associated with a cost object, such as a product. The price charged for a product must cover its long-run cost if the organization is to replace the capacity used to make the product when the capacity deteriorates.

Textbook **Exhibits 3-4A** and **3-4B** provide data on the cost for a medium to large firm to build its first e-commerce web site. Hardware and software costs are small in comparison to labor costs. Opportunity cost is also substantial.

The textbook example on **Fred's Grocery Stores** provides an extended example of how organizations create costs. Compare the section on "Starting Up" to Chapter 2's discussion of an organization's choice of target customers, and key success factors of service, quality, and price. The "Early Growth" section deals with capacity decisions and the organization's changing cost structure. The remaining sections discuss cost issues during the following stages: reaching the boundaries of existing capacity, expanding the product line and acquiring more capacity resources, redefining the business, and continued growth. The example's conclusion highlights the business risk created by business growth with large capacity-related costs.

VI. Cost Structures Today

A. The proportion of direct labor in the early 1900s could have been as high as 50% of unit product cost. Today, direct labor cost may be as small as 5% of unit product cost. The cost of direct materials, as earlier, may still constitute a substantial portion of manufacturing costs.

B. The proportion of capacity-related costs has increased because of the shift toward greater automation, the emphasis on better customer service, and the proliferation of multiple products. In addition, both flexible and capacity-related costs associated with design, product development, distribution, selling, marketing, and administrative activities have increased.

C. Cost systems designed for manufacturing activities with high direct labor content often used volume measures to allocate indirect costs. Such cost systems have become increasingly inaccurate in computing product costs as direct labor costs have become a small proportion of manufacturing cost, and indirect costs have correspondingly grown.

Textbook **Exhibit 3-5** uses information on Nanticoke Electric's cost structure to compute average profit for Nanticoke's customer groups. **Exhibit 3-6** shows how a simplified traditional volume-based cost system might allocate costs in determining profitability. When cost systems group costs that do not vary proportionally with volume, and then allocate them using a volume measure, the resulting costs are likely overstated or understated. Activity-based costing, described in the next section, provides a richer framework for analyzing costs.

> Learning Objective 1, continued:
> Explain why the appropriate derivation of a cost depends on how the cost will be used.

VII. Activity-Based Analysis of Costs

A. Types of Production Activities

1. **Unit-related activities** are those whose volume or level is proportional to the number of units produced or to other measures. Examples: direct labors, which are proportional to the number of units produced; energy required to operate manufacturing machinery, which is proportional to machine hours.

2. **Batch-related activities** are those triggered by the number of batches produced rather than by the number of units manufactured. Example: machine setups.

3. **Product-sustaining activities** are those that support the production and sale of individual products but are independent of actual production volumes and batches. Example: improving ice cream flavor recipes.

4. **Customer-sustaining activities**, which may pertain more to marketing and sales than to production, are those that enable the company to sell to an individual customer but are independent of the volume and mix of products sold and delivered to the customer. Example: technical support provided to individual customers.

5. **Business-sustaining activities** or **facility-sustaining activities** are those required for the basic functioning of the business or to provide the managerial infrastructure and support the upkeep of a plant. Examples: financial reporting and plant management. Activities such as advertising and conducting trade shows may be classified as *channel sustaining*. Business-sustaining, facility-sustaining, and channel-sustaining activity costs are not allocated to individual products, services, or customers.

6. **Other support activities** are activities beyond business-sustaining activities. The costs of these other support activities vary in proportion to the size or complexity of the organization and are allocated to cost objects in a way that reflects their cause.

The classification scheme of activities described above and diagrammed in textbook **Exhibit 3-7** is extremely important; we will return to it in Chapter 5 when we discuss activity-based costing systems and in Chapter 11 when we discuss forecasting and budgeting. The cost hierarchy can be used to develop a model of cost behavior for predicting costs or determining the costs for a cost object. Exhibit 3-7 indicates that unit, batch, product, and customer-sustaining activities are easily traced to the individual products, services, and customers for whom the activities are performed. In addition, the exhibit shows support costs that can be allocated to cost objects in a way that reflects their cause. The exhibit does *not* show channel-sustaining, facility-sustaining, and business-sustaining costs that are not allocated to cost objects.

B. Nonmanufacturing Costs as Product Costs

1. Nonmanufacturing costs, such as research and development, selling, and logistical activities, are large and growing in many organizations. The nonmanufacturing costs that have attracted the most attention are customer-related costs. These include the cost of selling the product to the customer, putting the product in the customer's hands, and providing after-sales support to the customer. Customer-related costs can be large and can vary widely across different customers.

2. Nonmanufacturing costs include both flexible and capacity-related components.

 Carefully work through the Orillia Novelty Plastics example and the associated textbook **Exhibits 3-8 through 3-11**. The example illustrates many of the concepts discussed in this chapter and highlights the clear difference between the cost of acquiring and the cost of using different resources.

Learning Objective 5: Explain the notion of life-cycle cost and how that idea is used in new product and product purchasing decisions.

VIII. Life-Cycle Costs

    A. **Life-cycle costing** is a systematic consideration of product costs during the product's lifetime. Organizations may consider life-cycle costing when deciding whether to introduce a product and for costing the product after the product has been introduced.

    B. Product Life-Cycle Phases

        1. **Product development and planning**: In this phase the organization incurs significant research and development costs and product testing costs.

        2. **Introduction**: In this phase the organization incurs significant promotional costs in introducing the product to the marketplace. At this stage the product's revenues may not cover the product's associated flexible and capacity-related costs to this point.

        3. **Growth**: In this phase the organization focuses on developing systems to deliver the product to the customer in the most effective way. There is often little or no price competition, and the product's revenues begin to cover the flexible and capacity-related costs incurred to produce, market, and distribute the product.

        4. **Product maturity**: In this phase the organization undertakes intense efforts to reduce costs to remain competitive and profitable. Price competition may become intense and lead to declining profit margins (the difference between the product's revenue and flexible costs).

        5. **Product decline and abandonment**: During this phase the market for the product declines and the product begins to become unprofitable. The organization may incur product abandonment costs, such as land reclamation in mining.

Not all products follow this same pattern, and product-related costs will occur unevenly over the product's lifetime. Note the discussion on the importance of considering the full range of costs: development, manufacturing, distribution, support, and abandonment. Life-cycle costing has little relevance for external reporting but has considerable importance for internal purposes.

 Textbook **Exhibit 3-12** displays resource use and cost information for Joan's Landscaping Services. **Exhibit 3-13** recasts Exhibit 3-1 by properly attributing capacity-related costs to the three product lines, resulting in different conclusions about how to improve the company's profitability. Joan should raise prices on the layout design business and increase volume in the two other product lines, which are high margin, to better use available capacity.

PRACTICE TEST QUESTIONS AND PROBLEMS

True/False

_____ 1. Flexible costs are always direct costs, but are sometimes treated as indirect costs.

_____ 2. Organizations should compute one set of costs and use the costs for both external financial statements and internal purposes.

_____ 3. The terms *costs* and *expenses* are always equivalent.

_____ 4. In manufacturing, direct costs are those that are traceable to the final product.

_____ 5. Under traditional functional cost classifications, manufacturing costs include distribution costs.

_____ 6. Because accurate information is so critical in today's competitive environment, organizations should pursue improved information systems no matter what the cost.

_____ 7. Manufacturing cost systems that use volume measures to allocate indirect costs can create very inaccurate product costs.

_____ 8. Unit-related activities are those whose volume is associated with the number of units produced.

_____ 9. The nonmanufacturing costs that have attracted the most attention for analysis are customer-related costs.

_____ 10. For external reporting purposes, all nonmanufacturing costs are treated as period costs and are reported as expenses.

Multiple-Choice

1. With respect to cost calculations, all of the following apply to generally accepted accounting principles (GAAP), EXCEPT:
   (a) focus on process rather than the decision relevance of the resulting cost allocations.
   (b) seek costs that are computed consistently through time and across different organizations.
   (c) highlight opportunity costs.
   (d) treat research and development costs as period costs.

2. Period costs include those
   (a) incurred for the manufacture of a product.
   (b) whose benefits cannot be matched easily with the products of a specific period.
   (c) that are directly traceable to a product.
   (d) incurred to pay direct labor workers.

3. Product costs are those
   (a) that are only indirectly traceable to a product.
   (b) that include selling costs of the good produced.
   (c) that include only manufacturing overhead.
   (d) incurred for the manufacture of a product.

4. Nonmanufacturing costs include each of the following, EXCEPT
   (a) direct materials costs.
   (b) distribution costs.
   (c) marketing costs.
   (d) general administrative costs.

5. In a car manufacturing firm using a traditional cost accounting system for external reporting, manufacturing costs include each of the following, EXCEPT
   (a) the cost of steel for each automobile chassis.
   (b) the cost of tires for each car.
   (c) the cost of janitorial services in the factory.
   (d) the cost of design engineers who designed the cars that are manufactured.

6. The composition of manufacturing costs has changed substantially since the early 1900s for all of the following reasons, EXCEPT:
   (a) the introduction of activity-based costing.
   (b) an increase in support activities required by a proliferation of multiple products.
   (c) an emphasis on better customer service.
   (d) a shift toward greater automation.

7. Which of the following is an indirect cost?
   (a) Cost of wood if the cost object is a wooden bookshelf
   (b) Cost of a production manager's salary when the manager oversees production of 20 products; the cost object is a specific motor
   (c) An instructor's salary when the instructor was hired to teach only one course; the cost object is the course the instructor will teach
   (d) Cost of leather if the cost object is a pair of leather shoes

8. Product-sustaining activities include all of the following, EXCEPT
   (a) maintenance of drawings and machine routings for parts.
   (b) engineering efforts to perform product enhancements.
   (c) obtaining patents.
   (d) machine setups.

9. Which of the following is a flexible cost?
   (a) Depreciation on a factory building
   (b) Cost of electrical power used to operate machinery
   (c) Salary of a plant manager
   (d) Cost of a climate-control warehouse

10. The five distinct stages of a typical product's life cycle include all of the following, EXCEPT:
    (a) product development and planning.
    (b) growth.
    (c) variance analysis.
    (d) product decline and abandonment.

Completion

1. A _____ _____ is a cost of a resource or activity that is acquired for or used by a single cost object.

2. Cost is defined as the monetary value of goods and services expended to obtain current or _____ benefits.

3. Manufacturing costs include all costs of _____ raw materials into finished product.

4. One notable change in manufacturing cost structure today is that the share of _____-_____ costs has become increasingly important.

5. Traditional accounting systems classified activities into those that varied with volume and those that did not. A richer framework for classifying activities in an organization uses the following categories: _____ _____, _____ _____, _____ _____, _____ _____, and _____ _____ activities.

6. _____ _____ resources are acquired and paid for in advance of when the work is done.

7. Labor costs may be treated as _____ costs because workers are paid in proportion to the hours they work. Conversely, labor costs may be treated as _____-_____ costs because the workers' wages are guaranteed to be paid in the short run, regardless of whether work is available.

8. The portion of product costs assigned to the products and sold in a period appears as _____ ____ _____ _____ expense on the income statement; the remaining portion of the product costs appears as an _____ on the _____ _____.

9. _____ _____ is the amount of lost profit when the opportunity afforded by one alternative is sacrificed to pursue another alternative.

10. The five distinct stages in a typical product's life cycle are the _____ _____ and planning phase, _____ phase, _____ phase, _____ _____ phase, and product decline and _____ phase.

Problems

1. Pat Hashimoto decided to quit her office job to start a produce-delivery business. Pat's office job paid $35,000 per year. Initially, Pat ran the business out of her parents' home and garage, though she did incur extra telephone charges that included a call answering service. She also produced flyers, which she posted in the neighborhoods she felt it would be feasible to deliver to. Pat delivered the produce using an old vehicle with negligible value. The business proved successful, and in time, Pat's customers requested nonperishable goods as well. Pat rented a warehouse to store nonperishable items.

   REQUIRED:

   Assuming the cost object is an item sold to a customer, determine whether each of the following costs is a capacity-related, flexible, direct, indirect, or opportunity cost of operating the business.

   (a) Pat's former salary of $35,000 per year

   (b) Telephone charges

   (c) Cost of flyers

   (d) Cost of produce

   (e) Cost of nonperishable goods

   (f) Warehouse rent

2. For many years, Kurtz Company has estimated its indirect manufacturing costs as 88% of its direct labor cost. The company's owner was concerned that the estimation might be very inaccurate because the manufacturing technology and process have changed, and direct labor cost is now a small proportion of manufacturing cost. Consequently, the owner asked the plant controller to analyze the activities at the plant in detail. The controller found that indirect manufacturing costs were incurred to perform activities

related to machine setup, inspecting finished products, and shipping products. She developed the following equation to estimate indirect manufacturing costs:

Indirect manufacturing costs = $0.70 × direct labor cost
+ $40 × number of setups
+ $23 × number of inspections
+ $34 × number of shipments

Planned activities for June and July are as follows:

	Direct labor cost	Number of setups	Number of inspections	Number of shipments
June	15,000	20	15	30
July	21,500	26	18	35

(a) Estimate the expected amount of indirect manufacturing costs for June and for July using the old equation based only on direct labor cost.

(b) Estimate the expected amount of indirect manufacturing costs for June and for July using the new equation developed by the controller.

(c) Why is there a difference between the two estimates? Which estimate is likely to be more accurate? Why?

SOLUTIONS TO PRACTICE TEST QUESTIONS AND PROBLEMS

True/False

1. True. Flexible costs are always direct costs, but are sometimes treated as indirect costs if it is inconvenient to account for them as direct costs and the cost is only a small part of total costs. For example, the cost of thread in a shirt might be treated as an indirect cost even though it is a flexible cost.

2. False. GAAP for external reporting promotes costs computed consistently through time and across organizations. For internal purposes, the nature of a decision defines the nature of the required cost, the way it should be computed, and the value of any cost number. A cost number that is useful for one decision may be useless for another decision.

3. False. Costs and expenses can be the same, but not in every situation. For example, costs associated with goods produced but not sold appear as an asset on the balance sheet; the costs appear as expenses on the income statement when the goods are sold.

4. True. In manufacturing product costing, this is the definition of direct costs.

5. False. Distribution costs are marketing costs and come under the general heading of nonmanufacturing costs.

6. False. The costs and benefits of the improved information should be assessed, at least intuitively.

7. True. When manufacturing cost systems groups costs that do not vary proportionally with volume, then allocate them using a volume measure, the resulting costs are likely overstated or understated. Activity-based costing provides a more accurate framework for analyzing costs.

8. True. This is the definition of unit-related activities.

9. True. Customer-related costs include the cost of selling the product to the customer, putting the product in the customer's hands, and providing after-sales support to the customer. Customer-related costs can be large and can vary widely across different customers.

10. True. For external reporting purposes, nonmanufacturing costs are treated as period costs and are reported as expenses, usually without the detailed analysis performed on manufacturing costs.

Multiple-Choice

1. c. Opportunity costs are used for analysis within the organization and do not appear in external financial statements.

2. b. This is the definition of period costs.

3. d. This is the definition of product costs.

4. a. Direct materials cost is a manufacturing cost.

5. d. Responses (a) and (b) are classified as direct materials, and response (c) is classified as an indirect manufacturing cost. For external reporting, response (d) is classified as a nonmanufacturing (period) cost.

6. a. Responses (b), (c), and (d) have contributed to an increase in capacity-related costs. Response (a), the introduction of activity-based costing, is a response to the substantial change in cost structure.

7. b. The production manager's salary is difficult to link to manufacture of a specific motor. Note that direct and indirect costs are defined with respect to a cost object.

8. d. Machine setups are considered a batch-related activity.

9. b. The remaining responses are capacity-related costs rather than flexible costs because the costs do not vary in proportion to production.

10. c. Variance analysis refers to computing and analyzing reasons for differences between actual and budgeted or standard costs.

Completion

1. direct cost

2. future

3. transforming

4. capacity-related

5. unit related, batch related, product sustaining, customer sustaining, business sustaining

6. Capacity-related

7. flexible, capacity-related

8. cost of goods sold, asset, balance sheet

9. Opportunity cost

10. product development, introduction, growth, product maturity, abandonment

Problems

1. (a) Opportunity cost
   (b) Indirect, capacity related
   (c) Indirect, capacity related
   (d) Direct, capacity related (because the perishable produce cannot be stored for long)
   (e) Direct, flexible (because nonperishable goods can be stored)
   (f) Indirect, capacity related

2. (a) Estimated indirect manufacturing costs based on direct labor cost:

   June: 0.88 × $15,000 = $13,200
   July: 0.88 × $21,500 = $18,920

   (b) Estimated indirect manufacturing costs based on the new equation:

   June: $0.7 × 15,000 + $40 × 20 + $23 × 15 + $34 × 30 = $12,665
   July: $0.7 × 21,500 + $40 × 26 + $23 × 18 + $34 × 35 = $17,694

   (c) The two estimates differ because the old equation does not reflect an understanding of how activities create costs. The estimates based on the new equation are more accurate because the equation relates activity usage to costs. Note that the sum of the costs for the two months under the old equation is not equivalent to the sum under the new equation.

chapter 4

Traditional Cost Management Systems

Learning Objectives

After reading this chapter, you will be able to

1. understand job order costing systems

2. understand how using job bid sheets is effective for estimating product costs in a job order costing system

3. use cost driver rates to apply support activity costs to products

4. discuss why cost systems with multiple cost driver rates give different cost estimates than cost systems with a single rate

5. evaluate a cost system to understand whether it is likely to distort product costs, explain the importance of recording actual costs, and compare them with estimated costs

6. appreciate the importance of conversion costs and the measurement of costs in multistage continuous-processing industries

7. understand the significance of differences between job order costing and multi-stage-process costing systems

8. understand the two-stage allocation process and service department allocation methods

SUMMARY

This chapter focuses on measuring the costs of products, services, and customers using two traditional cost management systems: job order costing and process costing. Job order costing systems often correspond to manufacturing for customized production. Process costing systems often correspond to manufacturing homogeneous products. Both types of cost systems assign some costs directly to units of product and assign manufacturing support costs to products on the basis of cost driver rates. The cost driver rates should be determined as the normal cost per unit of capacity of support activity available. Basing the cost driver rate on actual or budgeted activity levels that fluctuate over time may lead to understated or overstated costs. Cost distortions may also arise when multiple cost drivers cause support costs but the cost system assigns support costs using a single cost driver rate.

REVIEW OF KEY TERMS AND CONCEPTS

> Learning Objective 1: Understand job order costing systems.

I. Job Order and Process Costing Systems

  A. A **job order costing system** is a system for estimating costs of manufacturing products for different jobs required for specific customer orders. For example, a company that produces custom orders will use a job order costing system.

  B. A **process costing system** is a costing method that applies when all units produced during a specified time frame are treated as one unit of output. A key feature is homogeneity of the products.

  C. Categories of Inventories

    1. **Raw materials inventory**: Manufacturing material inputs on hand for production. Raw materials inventory valuation is the purchase cost of the inputs.

    2. **Work-in-process (WIP) inventory**: Goods only partially completed. WIP inventory valuation is the cost of the resources for jobs not yet completed.

    3. **Finished goods inventory**: Inventory that has been completed but not yet sold.

> Learning Objective 2: Understand how using job bid sheets is effective for estimating product costs in a job order costing system.

II. Components of a Job Bid Sheet

 Textbook **Exhibit 4-1** provides an example of a job bid sheet. Note panels 2 and 3 for standard engineering and industrial engineering specifications.

A. A **job bid sheet** is a format for estimating job costs. The textbook example has five distinct panels.

1. Panel 1: Customer, product, and number of units required.

2. Panel 2: Material quantities and prices

3. Panel 3: Direct labor hours and rates

Learning Objective 3: Use cost driver rates to apply support activity costs to products.
---

4. Panel 4: Manufacturing support activity costs based on cost driver rates. A **cost driver rate** is a ratio of normal cost for a support activity to normal level of cost driver for the activity.

5. Panel 5: Total costs estimated for the job, obtained by adding the total direct materials, total direct labor, and total support costs.

B. **Job costs** are the total of direct material, direct labor, and support activity costs estimated for, or identified with, a job.

C. **Margin** is the amount of profit added to estimated job costs to arrive at a **bid price**.

D. The **markup rate**, which is the ratio of the markup amount to the estimated costs for a job, may be contingent on the rate of return that the organization has specified. The **rate of return** is the ratio of net income to investment, also called *return on investment*. The markup rate may differ across product groups and market segments and may change over time.

Learning Objective 3, continued: Use cost driver rates to apply support activity costs to products.

Learning Objective 4: Discuss why cost systems with multiple cost driver rates give different estimates than cost systems with a single rate.

Traditional Cost Management Systems 51

E. Determining cost driver rates has become increasingly important because support costs now constitute a large portion of total costs in many industries. Moreover, many firms now recognize that several different factors may be driving (causing) support costs.

F. A **cost pool** is a subset of total support costs that can be associated with a distinct cost driver.

G. The **cost driver rate** is the rate at which support activity costs are applied to individual jobs. It is the ratio of the normal cost for a support activity accumulated in a cost pool to the normal level of the cost driver for the activity.

H. Determining a cost driver rate as the budgeted (or actual) cost per unit of the budgeted (or actual) use of that activity results in misleading product costs that can lead to a *death spiral*. The cost driver rate is best computed as described in G above.

Textbook **Exhibit 4-2** illustrates how cost driver rates can fluctuate if they are based on actual activity levels.

I. A general principle in selecting the **number of cost pools** is that separate cost pools should be used if the productivity of resources is different and if the pattern of demand varies across resources.

Make sure that you understand these concepts before proceeding. A comprehensive illustration of how to evaluate a cost system is provided via the Melissa's Auto Service example. Study this example carefully, paying particular attention to **Exhibits 4-3 through 4-7**. **Exhibit 4-8** displays the trade-offs in choosing the accuracy level of a product costing system.

Learning Objective 5: Evaluate a cost system to understand whether it is likely to distort product costs, explain the importance of recording actual costs, and compare them with estimated costs.

III. Recording Actual Job Costs

A. A **materials requisition note** informs the stores (materials storage) department to issue specified quantities of materials to the shop floor in order to commence production.

B. **Worker time cards** record the hours spent by each worker each day or week on different jobs.

C. A **job cost sheet** is a format for recording actual job costs.

Exhibits 4-9, 4-10, and **4-11** provide examples of each of the documents discussed above.

    D.   Actual costs can be compared to estimated costs to determine whether variations occurred in the quantity or prices of the resources used.

> Learning Objective 6: Appreciate the importance of conversion costs and the measurement of costs in multistage continuous-processing industries.

> Learning Objective 7: Understand the significance of differences between job order costing and multistage-process costing systems.

IV.   Multistage-Process Costing Systems

    A.   A **multistage-process costing system** is a system for determining product costs in multistage processing industries such as chemicals, basic metals, and pharmaceuticals. Multistage-process costing systems may also be used in some discrete-parts manufacturing plants such as those producing automobile components, small appliances, and electronic equipment.

    B.   A common feature of process costing is that the products that are produced are relatively **homogeneous**. Because few and relatively small differences occur in the production requirements for batches of different products, it is not necessary to keep separate cost records for individual jobs.

    C.   Because costs are measured only at process stages, **cost variances** are determined only at the level of the process stages.

    D.   With this method the first step is to **assess costs for each stage of the process** and then to assign costs to individual products.

    E.   Multistage-process costing systems and job order costing systems have the same ultimate objective: assign material, labor, and manufacturing support activity costs to products.

    F.   **Conversion costs** are costs of production labor and support activities to convert the materials or product at each process stage.

 Exhibits 4-13 through 4-15 illustrate process costing. **Exhibit 4-12** summarizes the differences between job order and process costing.

V. Appendix 4-1: Service Department Cost Allocations

SUMMARY

This appendix describes the direct allocation, sequential allocation, and reciprocal allocation methods of allocating service department costs to production departments. The appendix discusses conventional methods of allocation and how departmental structure affects allocation methods.

> Learning Objective 8: Understand the two-stage allocation process and service department allocation methods.

A. The Two-Stage Cost Allocation Method: First, expenses are assigned to production departments. Second, production department expenses are assigned to products.

B. The Effect of Departmental Structure on Allocation

1. Many plants are organized into departments that perform designated activities. **Production departments** are those directly responsible for converting raw materials into finished products. Examples include casting, stamping, machining, assembly, and packing departments.

2. **Service departments** perform activities that support production, but are not responsible for any of the conversion stages. Examples include machine maintenance, machine setup, and production scheduling. All service department costs are indirect support activity costs (with respect to products) because they do not arise from direct production activities.

Study **Exhibit 4-16** carefully, as it forms the basis for the next section of this appendix.

C. The Two-Stage Method

1. Conventional product costing systems assign indirect costs to products or jobs in two stages.

2. Step 1 of **Stage 1** identifies or estimates the normal manufacturing support costs (indirect costs) incurred in each production and service department. Step 2 of **Stage 1** then allocates all service department costs to the production departments. Conventional costing systems are based on the assumption that we cannot obtain direct measures of use of service departments' resources on individual jobs as conveniently as we can of production departments' resources.

3. The simplest **Stage 1 allocation method** is the **direct allocation method**. This method allocates service department costs to production departments by ignoring interdependencies between service departments.

Follow the PATIENTAID example to understand Stage 1 cost allocations using direct allocation of service department costs to production departments. **Exhibits 4-17 through 4-21** illustrate the process.

4. In **Stage 2**, the system assigns all of the accumulated indirect costs for production departments to individual products or jobs, using cost driver rates. Conventional allocation bases for production departments often are unit-based measures, including the number of units produced, the number of direct labor hours, direct labor cost, and the number of machine hours.

Stage 2 allocations are illustrated in the PATIENTAID example in **Exhibits 4-22 through 4-25**.

D. Distortions Caused by Two-Stage Allocations: There are two major reasons why two-stage allocations can distort product costs.

1. Allocations are based on unit-related measures.

2. Consumption ratios of resources for products often are different from those based on unit-related measures.

Note in **Exhibit 4-26** that A is produced in larger batch sizes than B is. Because the two products require the same number of machine hours per unit, both A and B will be allocated the same support costs, even though B requires more setups.

E. **The sequential allocation method** is a method that recognizes interdependencies between service departments and allocates service department costs, one service department at a time, in sequential order.

1. Companies use the sequential method when there is no pair of service departments in which each department in that pair consumes a significant proportion of the services produced by the other department in that pair.

2. The sequential allocation method arranges service departments in order, so that a service department receives costs allocated from another service department only before its own costs have been allocated to other departments. Once a service department's costs have been allocated, no costs of other departments are allocated back to it.

Exhibits **4-27** and **4-28** illustrate the sequential allocation method.

F. **The reciprocal allocation method** is a method to determine service department cost allocations simultaneously, recognizing the reciprocity between pairs of service departments. The method involves setting up and solving simultaneous equations that describe the resource consumption.

 Exhibit 4-27 is modified to produce **Exhibit 4-29** to illustrate the reciprocal method. **Exhibit 4-30** shows the reciprocally allocated costs. Note that Exhibit 4-30's total production department costs after the allocations differ from those in Exhibit 4-28 developed under the sequential allocation method.

G. Development of an activity-based cost system, as described in the next chapter, usually eliminates the need for the second step in Stage 1 allocations.

PRACTICE TEST QUESTIONS AND PROBLEMS

True/False

_____ 1. A job order costing system is a common method for estimating product costs in the chemicals industry.

_____ 2. Standard engineering specifications appear on a job bid sheet.

_____ 3. Markup and margin are two different concepts.

_____ 4. Determination of cost driver rates based on planned or actual short-term usage produces misleading product costs.

_____ 5. A general principle in selecting the number of cost pools is that separate cost pools should be used if the productivity of resources is different and if the pattern of demand varies across resources.

_____ 6. Worker time cards record total hours worked for each worker without reference to the specific jobs on which they work.

_____ 7. Multistage-process costing systems are used in the pharmaceuticals industry.

_____ 8. In process costing, separate records are kept for individual jobs.

_____ 9. (Appendix) In manufacturing plants, service departments are those performing activities that support production, but are not responsible for any of the conversion stages.

_____ 10. (Appendix) The direct allocation, sequential allocation, and reciprocal allocation methods all take interactions with other service departments into account.

Multiple-Choice

1. Each of the following statements is true about job order costing systems, EXCEPT:
   (a) a job order costing system is a method used for estimating product costs in firms that have several distinct products.
   (b) a job order costing system estimates costs of manufacturing products for different jobs required for customer orders.
   (c) a job order costing system provides the means to estimate costs so that bids can be prepared.
   (d) a job order costing system relies on the concept of conversion costs.

2. From the following information determine a price incorporating a 15% markup on job EC1. For EC1, direct materials are $3,000, direct labor is $2,500, and support activity costs are $4,700.
   (a) $ 6,325
   (b) $ 8,855
   (c) $ 8,280
   (d) $11,730

3. Determine the cost driver rate for cost pool ABC from the following information: The required rate of return is 18%; normal cost of support activities is $8,700, the markup percentage is 12%, and the normal level of the cost driver is 225.
   (a) $38.67
   (b) $1,044.00
   (c) $48,333.33
   (d) $27.00

4. The correct method of determining cost driver rates
   (a) uses the previous year's actual cost per unit of the activity.
   (b) estimates the normal cost per unit of the activity level committed.
   (c) estimates the actual cost per unit of the planned usage level of the activity.
   (d) estimates the actual cost per unit of the activity level committed.

5. A materials requisition note
   (a) instructs shop floor personnel to request materials from its suppliers.
   (b) informs the customer that materials for use in producing their product has been delayed.
   (c) instructs stores to issue materials to the shop floor to commence production.
   (d) is a note from stores to suppliers to ship more materials.

6. Each of the following is essential to recording actual job costs, EXCEPT
   (a) a materials requisition note.
   (b) a stores department quality check form.
   (c) worker time cards.
   (d) a job cost sheet.

7. Each of the following is a major type of inventory category used in traditional manufacturing cost systems, EXCEPT
    (a) finished goods inventory.
    (b) cost of goods sold.
    (c) raw materials.
    (d) work-in-process.

8. Process costing is suitable for each of the following manufacturing operations, EXCEPT
    (a) oil refining.
    (b) pharmaceuticals.
    (c) automobile components.
    (d) specialty printing jobs.

9. (Appendix) In stage one of the conventional cost allocation procedure, the first step is to
    (a) assess actual support costs for each department.
    (b) estimate normal support costs for each department.
    (c) allocate all service department support costs to production departments.
    (d) allocate production department costs to individual products.

10. (Appendix) Satellite Company has total support costs of $480,000. It uses a conventional cost accounting system and has 5 service departments and 5 production departments, which produce 25 different products. Ultimately, how much of the $480,000 will NOT be allocated down to the product level?
    (a) $ 48,000
    (b) $480,000
    (c) $ 1,920
    (d) $ 0

Completion

1. A job bid sheet is a format for _____ _____ costs.

2. The cost driver rate is the ratio of the _____ cost for a support activity to the _____ level of the cost _____ for the activity.

3. A _____ _____ note lists the materials required to commence production.

4. _____ is the amount of profit added to estimated job costs to arrive at a bid price.

5. A _____ _____ is a subset of total support costs that can be associated with a distinct cost driver.

6. In a multistage-process costing system the first step is to determine costs for each _____ of the process and then assign the costs to products.

7. In process costing settings, the common feature is that the products manufactured are all relatively _____

8. _____ _____ are the costs of production labor and support activities to convert the materials or product at each process stage.

9. (Appendix) Conventional costing systems assume that we cannot obtain _____ measures of the use of service departments' resources on individual jobs as conveniently as we can for production departments.

10. (Appendix) The _____ _____ method is a simple method that allocates service department costs directly to the production departments, ignoring interactions among other service departments.

Problems

1. The MPC Company has stamping and assembly departments. MPC uses a single predetermined cost driver rate based on plantwide direct labor hours. The cost estimates for 2000 are as follows:

	Stamping	Assembly	Total
Manufacturing support	$80,000	$28,000	$108,000
Direct labor hours	4,000	7,000	11,000
Machine hours	6,000	4,000	10,000

   (a) Determine the plantwide (single predetermined) cost driver rate for 2000.

   (b) Determine departmental cost driver rates based on machine hours for stamping and direct labor hours for assembly. That is, assume that the cost pool of stamping manufacturing support is assigned based on stamping's machine hours and that the cost pool of assembly manufacturing support is assigned based on assembly's direct labor hours.

2. Blasto Company produces and sells a variety of chemical products. The inputs are combined in the mixing department and then packed in quart-sized canisters in the packaging department. The following information pertains to the B100 mixing department for June.

Item	Price per Quart	Quarts
Input X	$0.10	20,000
Input Y	0.20	30,000
Input Z	0.25	10,000
B100		60,000

Conversion costs for the B100 mixing department are $0.50 per quart for June. Determine the cost per quart of B100 before packaging.

SOLUTIONS TO PRACTICE TEST QUESTIONS AND PROBLEMS

True/False

1. False. The chemicals industry uses process costing methods, as it is a continuous processing industry.

2. True. Job bid sheets contain standard engineering specifications for the materials required.

3. False. Both concepts relate to the amount of profit added to estimated job costs to arrive at a price. The markup rate is the ratio of the markup amount to the estimated costs for a job.

4. True. With such an approach, job costs appear to be higher when demand is lower, and vice versa. A "death spiral" can result if perceived higher costs lead to higher bid prices, causing even lower demand and higher cost driver rates.

5. True. This principle helps avoid the cost distortions arising when multiple cost drivers cause support costs but the cost system assigns support costs using a single cost driver rate.

6. False. Worker time cards specify hours spent on specific jobs.

7. True. The pharmaceuticals industry uses continuous processing because of the degree of homogeneity among its products.

8. False. In process costing it is unnecessary to keep separate records for individual jobs.

9. True. This is the definition of service departments in manufacturing plants.

10. False. The direct allocation method does not take interactions with other service departments into account.

Multiple-Choice

1. d. Job order costing does not rely on the concept of conversion costs.

2. d. Job cost for EC1 is the total of direct materials of $3,000, direct labor of $2,500 and support costs of $4,700, or $10,200. The markup is $10,200 × 15% = $1,530, resulting in a price of $10,200 + 1,530 = $11,730.

3. a. The cost driver rate for cost pool ABC equals the normal cost of support activity divided by the normal level of the cost driver, or $8,700/225 = $38.67.

4. b. The correct method of determining cost driver rates estimates the normal cost per unit of the activity level committed. The other methods may result in a "death spiral" in which overstated costs lead to noncompetitive prices.

5. c. A materials requisition note instructs stores to issue materials to the shop floor to commence production.

6. b. Stores department quality check forms (a fictitious form) are not used to record actual job costs.

7. b. Cost of goods sold is an expense on the income statement.

8. d. Job order costing is suitable for specialty printing jobs and other customized jobs. Process costing is often used with discrete-part manufacturing when the items are fairly homogeneous.

9. b. The first step is to estimate normal support costs for each department.

10. d. All of the $480,000 will be allocated down to the product level.

Completion

1. estimating job

2. normal, normal, driver

3. materials requisition

4. Margin

5. cost pool

6. stage

7. homogeneous

8. Conversion costs

9. direct

10. direct allocation

Problems

1. (a) Plantwide cost driver rate = $108,000/11,000 direct labor hours
        = $9.82 per direct labor hour

   (b) Departmental cost driver rates:

   Stamping department = $80,000/6,000 machine hours
                       = $13.34 per machine hour

   Assembly department = $28,000/7,000 direct labor hours
                       = $4 per direct labor hour

2.
Input X: $0.10 × 20,000	$2,000	
Input Y: $0.20 × 30,000	6,000	
Input Y: $0.25 × 10,000	2,500	$10,500
Conversion costs: $0.50 × 60,000		$30,000
Total costs:		$40,500
Number of quarts of B100		60,000
Cost per quart of B100		$0.68

chapter 5

Activity-Based Cost Management Systems

After reading this chapter, you will be able to

1. understand how traditional cost systems, using only unit-level drivers, distort product and customer costs
2. describe why factories producing a more varied and complex mix of products have higher costs than factories producing only a narrow range of products
3. design an activity-based cost system by linking resource costs to the activities performed and then to cost objects, such as products and customers
4. appreciate the role for choosing appropriate activity cost drivers when tracing activity costs to products and customers
5. use the information from a well-designed activity-based cost system to improve operations and make better decisions about products and customers
6. understand the importance of measuring the practical capacity of resources and the cost of unused capacity
7. assign marketing, distribution, and selling expenses to customers
8. analyze customer profitability
9. appreciate the role for activity-based cost systems for service companies
10. discuss the barriers for implementing activity-based cost systems and how these might be overcome

SUMMARY

This chapter explains how activity-based cost systems calculate costs more accurately than traditional cost systems based on unit-level drivers. Activity-based cost systems link resource costs to the activities performed, then to products, customers, or other cost objects. Appropriate cost driver rates are based on practical capacity of the resources supplied. Operational activity-based management uses activity-based cost information to identify promising opportunities for reducing costs in indirect and support activities. Strategic activity-based management uses activity-based cost information for decisions in such areas as pricing, distribution, product design, product mix, and minimum order sizes. The chapter concludes by describing reasons for potential resistance to implementing activity-based cost systems.

REVIEW OF KEY TERMS AND CONCEPTS

> Learning Objective 1: Understand how traditional cost systems, using only unit-level drivers, distort product and customer costs.

I. Traditional Manufacturing Cost Systems

    A. For many years, manufacturing companies used traditional manufacturing cost systems such as the job order and process costing systems described in Chapter 4. Indirect manufacturing costs were accumulated as support department expenses and then allocated to production departments, and then to products.

    B. Cooper Pen Company Cost System Example

        1. The company expanded its product line from high-volume blue and black pens to premium-priced red and purple pens.

        2. Introducing red and purple pens required more production changeovers, with an associated increase in several activities. Purchasing and scheduling activities also required more time.

        3. All the plant's indirect expenses were aggregated at the plant level and allocated to products based on their direct labor cost.

Exhibit 5-1 presents a product line profitability analysis based on Cooper Pen's original simple cost system. The bottom line of the exhibit prompted the company's controller to consider deemphasizing blue and black pens and to keep introducing new specialty colored pens.

> Learning Objective 2: Describe why factories producing a more varied and complex mix of products have higher costs than factories producing only a narrow range of products.

II. Limitations of Cooper Pen's Traditional Cost System

    A. Cooper Pen's New Manufacturing Environment

        1. Automation has reduced direct labor costs and increased indirect expenses.

2. The new products are custom, low-volume products requiring increased scheduling, setup, quality control, and other activities.

B. Traditional Cost Systems

1. **Production departments** are directly responsible for some of the work of converting raw materials into finished products. Examples include machining and assembly departments.

2. **Service departments** perform activities that support production but are not responsible for any of the conversion stages. Examples include machine maintenance, machine setup, and production scheduling. Service department costs are typically indirect support activity costs (with respect to products) because they do not arise directly from production activities.

3. Cooper Pen's cost system uses only a single cost center, the plant. Even if Cooper Pen used multiple production and service department cost centers, it would still encounter severe distortions in its reported product costs. Such cost systems usually used only unit-level drivers (such as direct labor dollars or direct labor hours) to allocate production center expenses to products.

4. The example on simple and complex pen factories illustrates how unit-level drivers lead to product cost distortion in an environment with high product variety. Such systems underestimate the cost of resources for specialty, low-volume products, and overestimate the cost of resources for high-volume, standard products.

Learning Objective 3: Design an activity-based cost system by linking resource costs to the activities performed and then to cost objects, such as products and customers.

Learning Objective 4: Appreciate the role for choosing appropriate activity cost drivers when tracing activity costs to products and customers.

Learning Objective 5: Use the information from a well-designed activity-based cost system to improve operations and make better decisions about products and customers.

III. Activity-Based Cost Management Systems

A. Product-cost distortions resulting from conventional two-stage systems can be overcome by designing an activity-based costing system. *Activity-based costing* first assigns resource costs to the activities performed by the organization. Then activity costs are assigned to cost objects, such as products, customers, and services, that benefit from or are creating the demand for activities.

B. **Activity-based cost (ABC) management systems** are systems based on activities; the systems link organizational spending on resources to the products and services produced and delivered to customers.

C. Tracing Costs to Activities

1. Develop the *activity dictionary*, the list of the major activities performed by the plant's human and physical resources. A useful guideline is to use verbs to describe activities.

2. Obtain information to assign resource expenses to each activity in the activity dictionary.

3. Keep in mind appropriate cost hierarchies in developing activity categories. The manufacturing hierarchy, for example, includes unit-level, batch-level, and product-sustaining activities.

4. **Operational activity-based management** is a system that uses information collected by the ABC system at the activity level to identify promising opportunities for reducing costs in indirect and support activities.

Exhibits 5-2 and **5-3** display Cooper Pen's activities and activity expenses and show how the resource expenses are mapped to the activities. The expenses in the last column of Exhibit 5-2 appear at the top of Exhibit 5-3 and are mapped to activities. Note that although costs have not yet been driven down to products, managers can use information at the activity level to identify promising opportunities for reducing costs in indirect and support activities. **Exhibit 5-4** reinforces the concept of transforming the focus from what money is spent on to activities provided by the purchased resources.

D. Tracing Costs from Activities to Products

1. **Activity cost drivers** are units of measurement for the level or quantity of the activity performed. Activity cost drivers identify the linkage between activities and cost objects.

2. An **activity cost driver rate** is the ratio of the cost of resources to provide an activity to the level of the capacity made available by those resources.

3. A **bill of activities** is the set of activities and costs associated with individual products. A bill of activities can provide insights into ways that managers can transform unprofitable products into profitable ones.

4. **Strategic activity-based management (ABM)** involves decisions in such areas as pricing, distribution, product design, product mix, and minimum order sizes. Recall that **activity-based management (ABM)** is an approach to operations control that involves the five-step process of identifying the process objectives, charting activities, classifying activities, continuously improving processes, and eliminating activities whose costs exceed their value.

Exhibit 5-5 displays measures of Cooper Pen's activity cost drivers. **Exhibit 5-6** computes activity cost driver rates using activity expenses calculated in Exhibit 5-3 and total activity cost driver information in Exhibit 5-5. **Exhibit 5-7** assigned activity expenses to products, and **Exhibit 5-8** uses the information in Exhibit 5-7 to compute product profitability for each of the pen lines. Contrast the profitability assessment in Exhibit 5-7 with the assessment in Exhibit 5-1, which is based on Cooper Pen's traditional cost system.

E. Selecting Activity Cost Drivers

1. The selection of an activity cost driver involves a subjective trade-off between accuracy and the cost of measurement. Data requirements must also be considered in choosing the number of activity cost drivers.

2. **Transaction drivers** count how often an activity is performed. Transaction drivers are the least expensive type of cost driver but are also the least accurate, because they assume that the same quantity of resources is required every time an activity is performed. Examples: number of setups and number of receipts.

3. **Duration drivers** represent the amount of time required to perform an activity. Duration drivers are appropriate when significant variation exists in the amount of activity required for different outputs. Examples: setup hours and inspection hours.

4. **Intensity drivers** directly charge for the resources used each time an activity is performed. These drivers are the most accurate activity cost drivers but are also the most expensive to implement because they require direct charging via a job order costing system. Intensity drivers should be used only when the resources associated with performing an activity are both expensive and variable each time an activity is performed.

5. ABC analysts may simulate an intensity driver with a *weighted index* approach. Individuals estimate the relative difficulty of performing the task for one type of product or customer versus another.

> Learning Objective 6: Understand the importance of measuring the practical capacity of resources and the cost of unused capacity.

IV. Measuring the Cost of Resource Capacity

  A. **Practical capacity** is the amount of work that can be performed by resources supplied for production or service.

  B. Activity cost driver rates should be calculated as the cost of supplied resources divided by the practical capacity of work that it could perform. In this way, the activity cost driver rate will reflect the underlying efficiency of the process.

  C. **Cost of unused capacity** is an expense determined by the amount of resources left unused after production. The cost of unused capacity should not be assigned to products produced or customers served during a period. Instead, the cost should be assigned to the level in the organization where decisions are made that affect the supply of capacity resources and the demand for those resources. The cost assignment will provide feedback to the affected manager on supply and demand decisions.

  D. Fixed and Variable Costs in ABC Systems

    1. An ABC system does not assume that indirect costs assigned to products or customers will vary based on short-term changes in activity volumes.

    2. Committed costs become variable via a two-step procedure:

        a. Demands for resources change.

        b. Managers make decisions to increase or decrease the supply of committed resources to meet the new level of demand for activities provided by the resources.

    3. Unused capacity can be managed out of the system in two ways:

        a. Increase the volume of business.

        b. Reduce the supply of unused resources.

> Learning Objective 7: Assign marketing, distribution, and selling expenses to customers.

V. Marketing, Selling, and Distribution Expenses: Tracking Costs to Customers

   A. Many conventional systems exclude marketing, selling, distribution, and other nonmanufacturing costs from product costs or use arbitrary methods, such as relative sales value, to assign them.

   B. With today's emphasis on customer satisfaction and market-oriented strategies, the costs of marketing, selling, and distribution expenses have been increasing rapidly.

   C. ABC analysis of marketing, selling, and distribution costs will reveal profitable and unprofitable customers and reveal the financial impact of serving customers. The largest customers are likely to be among the company's most profitable or its most unprofitable.

Exhibit 5-9 provides an example of an activity dictionary and activity cost drivers for marketing, selling, and distribution activities. Note the variety of driver types: intensity drivers, transaction activity cost drivers, and duration drivers. Also note the implicit customer cost hierarchy that includes, for example, order-related activities and customer-sustaining activities. The display above Exhibit 5-9 illustrates an activity-based costing customer profitability analysis that incorporates ABC information developed using Exhibit 5-9.

> Learning Objective 8: Analyze customer profitability.

VI. Managing Customer Profitability

Exhibit 5-10 classifies customers into four broad groups characterized by various combinations of ABC-derived cost to serve and profit (net ABC margin realized). The diagram shows that companies can enjoy profitable customers in different ways and highlights the benefits of ABC identification of low-margin, high-cost-to-serve customers for management attention.

   A. *Low margin, low cost to serve.* The cost of serving may be low because the customer places large orders for standard products, with predictable delivery schedules and EDI technology.

   B. *High margin, high cost to serve.* The cost of serving may be high because of small orders and heavy technical support.

C. *High margin, low cost to serve.* These customers may be vulnerable to competition.

D. *Low margin, high cost to serve.* These customers are the most challenging. The company can work with the customer to develop less costly ways to serving the customer.

Learning Objective 9: Appreciate the role for activity-based cost systems for service companies.

VII. Service Companies

A. Service companies are often ideal candidates for activity-based costing.

1. Most costs are indirect and appear to be fixed.

2. In many service industries, the variable cost for an incremental transaction is essentially zero.

B. The variation in demand for organizational resources is much more customer driven in service organizations than in manufacturing organizations. Product manufacturing costs are independent of how customers use the product. In contrast, customer behavior determines the basic operating costs of products. For example, some checking account customers may maintain a high cash balance and make few deposits and withdrawals, whereas other customers maintain a low cash balance and make many deposits and withdrawals.

C. A company's managers should understand all the relationships it has with a customer and act based on total relationship profitability.

D. The principles for developing an activity-based cost system for a service company are identical to those followed in manufacturing companies.

 Exhibit 5-11 displays activities and associated activity cost drivers used in an ABC study of a bank.

Learning Objective 10: Discuss the barriers for implementing activity-based cost systems and how these might be overcome.

VIII. Implementation Issues

A. Lack of Clear Business Purpose

1. ABC projects should be launched with a specific business purpose, such as to redesign or improve processes, influence product design decisions, rationalize product mix, or better manage customer relationships. In conjunction with identifying the business purpose, the project team should identify which manager's or department's behavior and decisions will change as a consequence of the ABC information.

2. The primary purpose of the model will influence the design of the initial model. A model intended primarily for process improvement will differ from a model intended for improving customer relationship management.

3. Do not initiate an ABC project with merely a vague statement that ABC will provide a "more accurate cost system."

4. Do not oversell ABC's capabilities. That is, do not promise that ABC will solve all the business unit's costing and financial problems.

B. Lack of Senior Management Commitment

1. The organization's senior line managers should fully support the ABC project because these managers have the power to make decisions about such items as processes, product designs, product mix, pricing, and customer relationships.

2. Multifunctional project teams not only provide broad expertise to incorporate into the ABC model, but also can build support for the project across various departments and groups.

C. Delegating the Project to Consultants

1. ABC consultants and ABC software can provide valuable assistance for organizations, but are not a substitute for overcoming other potential pitfalls.

2. Consultants may have limited familiarity with a company's operations and business problems.

3. Consultants cannot build management consensus and support to make decisions with the ABC information.

D. Poor ABC Model Design

1. ABC model design involves continual appropriate trade-offs so the essential function of the system can be accomplished at minimal additional cost.

2. Project teams may build overcomplex models. Such models are too complicated to build and maintain, and too complex for managers to understand and act upon.

3. Project teams may misidentify causal relationships between cost objects, activities, and resources.

E. Individual and Organizational Resistance to Change

1. Resistance arises when people feel threatened by the suggestion that their work could be improved or past decisions were unwise.

2. Nonovert resistance includes ignoring the ABC information or asking for unnecessary further development work.

3. Overt resistance includes rejecting the ABC approach or the project team's motives.

PRACTICE TEST QUESTIONS AND PROBLEMS

True/False

_____ 1. In manufacturing plants, service departments are those performing activities that support production, but are not responsible for any of the conversion stages.

_____ 2. Using multiple production and service department cost centers will prevent severe cost distortions in reported product costs.

_____ 3. Distortions from two-stage allocations occur when the link between the cause for support costs and the basis for assignment of costs to individual products is broken.

_____ 4. In activity-based costing, service department costs are allocated to production departments before they are assigned to individual jobs or products.

_____ 5. An important difference between conventional and activity-based costing systems is that activity-based systems do not rely solely on unit-based measures to assign costs to products.

_____ 6. The only way that unused capacity can be managed out of a system is to reduce the supply of unused resources.

_____ 7. Activity-based costing's primary usefulness is in manufacturing, rather than service contexts.

_____ 8. Activity cost drivers always represent the amount of time required to perform an activity.

_____ 9. Organizations should always discontinue serving customers who are associated with low margins and are high cost to serve.

_____ 10. The benefits to activity-based costing are so clear that organizations rarely face resistance in implementing activity-based costing.

Multiple-Choice

1. Which of the following four pairs of activities and cost drivers has the weakest link between activity and driver?

	Activity	**Allocation Basis**
(a)	Machine maintenance	Square feet of floor space
(b)	Lighting on shop floor	Number of kilowatt hours
(c)	Quality control	Number of inspections
(d)	Ordering of materials	Number of orders

2. Unit-related measures include all of the following, EXCEPT
   (a) number of units made.
   (b) number of direct labor hours.
   (c) number of machine hours.
   (d) number of material handlers.

3. Which of the following is NOT part of developing an activity-based cost system?
   (a) Use the reciprocal allocation method.
   (b) Develop an activity dictionary.
   (c) Obtain information to assign resource expenses to each activity in the activity dictionary.
   (d) Select activity cost drivers to trace costs from activities to products.

4. *Setup hours* is an example of a
   (a) duration driver.
   (b) intensity driver.
   (c) transaction driver.
   (d) weighted index approach.

5. Products R51 and R53 each are assigned $29 in support costs by a conventional accounting system. An activity analysis revealed that although subsequent production requirements are identical, R51 requires 30 minutes more setup time than R53. According to an activity-based costing system, R51 likely is _____ under the conventional accounting system.
   (a) undercosted
   (b) overcosted
   (c) fairly costed
   (d) accurately costed

6. Activity-based costing develops cost drivers that
    (a) do not take any support activities into account.
    (b) take only some production activities into account.
    (c) directly link the activities performed to the products produced.
    (d) indirectly link the activities performed to the products produced.

7. Ward Company produces six products. Under their conventional method of cost allocation using one cost driver, job AR6 costs $142.75. Activity-based costing was applied to all of Ward's products, and three cost drivers were found to be necessary. The new cost of AR6 was determined to be $133.00. Which of the following statements regarding product AR6 under activity-based costing is the most accurate?
    (a) AR6 is less accurately costed.
    (b) AR6 is more accurately costed.
    (c) AR6 will now command a much higher sales price.
    (d) AR6 will now command a much lower sales price.

8. Which of the following is not a marketing, selling, or distribution cost?
    (a) Order execution
    (b) Shipping
    (c) Sales catalog
    (d) Material purchasing

9. A key reason for an activity-based cost analysis of marketing, selling, and distribution costs is:
    (a) the cost of marketing, selling and distribution activities has been increasing rapidly.
    (b) generally accepted accounting principles now require it.
    (c) customers have demanded it.
    (d) controllers have demanded it.

10. Barriers for implementing activity-based cost systems include all of the following, EXCEPT
    (a) launching activity-based costing with a specific business purpose.
    (b) lack of senior management commitment.
    (c) delegating the project to consultants.
    (d) overcomplex activity-based cost models.

Completion

1. _____ activity-based _____ is a system that uses information collected by the ABC system at the activity level to identify promising opportunities for reducing costs in indirect and support activities.

2. Activity cost driver rates should be calculated as the cost of supplied resources divided by the _____ _____ of work that it could perform.

3. _____ activity-based management involves decisions in such areas as pricing, distribution, product design, product mix, and minimum order sizes.

4. _____ drivers count how often an activity is performed.

5. The variation in demand for organizational resources is much more _____-driven in service organization than in manufacturing organizations.

6. A company's managers should understand all the _____ it has with a customer and act based on total _____ profitability.

7. Specific business purposes for launching ABC projects include _____ processes, _____ product design decisions, or better managing customer _____.

8. ABC model design involves continual appropriate _____-_____ so the essential function of the system can be accomplished at minimal additional cost.

9. With conventional costing systems, products manufactured in _____ batches or in _____ annual volumes may be undercosted because batch-related and product-sustaining costs are assigned using unit-related drivers.

10. In the past, conventional cost systems either completely excluded marketing, selling, and distribution costs or assigned them to products on an _____ basis.

Problems

1. Determine a cost driver for each of the following activities:

    (a) Electricity
    _____

    (b) Purchasing
    _____

    (c) Equipment setups
    _____

    (d) Computer services
    _____

    (e) Plant depreciation
    _____

    (f) Janitorial service
    _____

    (g) Quality assurance
    _____

    (h) Administrative services
    _____

    (i) Shipping
    _____

(j)   Robot maintenance
_____

2.   ABC Company has determined the following information about support activity cost pools and cost drivers:

Cost Pool	Activity Costs	Cost Drivers
Machine setups	$250,000	4,000 setup hours
Material handling	80,000	25,000 lbs. of material
Inspection	30,000	2,000 inspections

The following information pertains to the manufacturing of Products TM3 and MP179:

	TM3	MP179
Number of units produced	3,000	5,000
Direct materials	$24,000	$32,000
Direct labor	$14,000	$18,000
Number of setup hours	100	120
Pounds of material used	3,000	4,500
Number of inspections	20	15

Determine the unit cost for each of the two products using an activity-based costing approach.

SOLUTIONS TO PRACTICE TEST QUESTIONS AND PROBLEMS

True/False

1.   True.   This is the definition of service departments in manufacturing plants.

2. False. Given diverse products or diverse customer requirements, if a cost system is based on unit-level drivers, the system is likely to report severely distorted product costs even if the system uses multiple product and service department cost centers.

3. True. When this link breaks, distortions occur.

4. False. In activity-based costing this step, associated with conventional product costing systems, is bypassed as activities are directly linked to products.

5. True. Activity-based systems also rely, for example, on batch-related and product-sustaining measures.

6. False. Unused capacity can also be managed out of the system by increasing the volume of business to use the capacity.

7. False. Activity-based costing is also extremely useful in service companies and in customer profitability analysis in manufacturing and service companies.

8. False. Activity cost drivers may also be based on how often an activity is performed or may directly charge for the resources used each time an activity is performed.

9. False. Organizations may work with such customers to develop lower-cost ways to serve the customers, for example.

10. False. Various factors can create resistance to any major change, including a change in cost system that may result in different evaluations of decisions or performance.

Multiple-Choice

1. a. The weakest link is between machine maintenance and floor space.

2. d. The number of material handlers is not a unit-related measure. That is, it is not directly related to number of units of product produced.

3. a. The reciprocal allocation method is used in conventional two-stage cost systems, not in activity-based cost systems.

4. a. A duration driver represents the amount of time required to perform an activity.

5. a. R51 is likely undercosted, as it is actually consuming more resources than R53, and both products receive the same cost assignment based on unit-level drivers.

6. c. ABC develops cost drivers that directly link the activities performed to the products produced.

7. b. Product AR6 is now more accurately costed, given the use of three cost drivers and the activity-based costing method.

8. d. Materials purchasing is a manufacturing cost, not a marketing, selling, or distribution cost.

9. a. Because these costs have been increasing rapidly and therefore represent a larger proportion of total costs, it is important to reflect the demand for the marketing, selling, and distribution activities needs in product costs for managerial purposes.

10. a. It is advisable to launch activity-based cost projects with a specific business purpose rather than a vague promise about the benefits of activity-based costing.

Completion

1. Operational, management

2. practical capacity

3. Strategic

4. Transaction

5. customer

6. relationships, relationship

7. improving (or redesigning), influencing, relationships

8. trade-offs

9. small, small

10. arbitrary

Problems

1. (a) Number of kilowatt hours
   (b) Number of orders
   (c) Number of setup or setup hours
   (d) Number of hours of service provided
   (e) Number of square feet
   (f) Number of square feet
   (g) Number of inspections or number of batches
   (h) Number of employees
   (i) Number of shipments
   (j) Number of robot hours

2.

Cost Pool	Activity Costs	Cost Drivers	Driver Rates
Machine setups	$250,000	4,000 hrs.	$62.50/hr
Material handling	80,000	25,000 lbs.	$ 3.20/lb.
Inspection	30,000	2,000 insp.	$15.00/insp.

	TM3	MP179
Direct materials	$24,000	$33,000
Direct labor	14,000	18,000
Support costs:		
Machine setups [$62.50 × 100 (120)]	6,250	7,500
Materials handling [$3.2 × 3,000 (4500)]	9,600	14,400
Inspection [$15 × 20 (15)]	300	225
Total manufacturing costs	$54,150	$72,125
Number of units produced	3,000	5,000
Unit cost	$18.05	$14.43

chapter 6

Management Accounting Information for Activity and Process Decisions

*L*earning *O*bjectives

After reading this chapter, you will be able to

1. explain why sunk costs are not relevant costs
2. analyze make-or-buy decisions
3. demonstrate the influence of qualitative factors in making decisions
4. compare the different types of facilities layouts
5. explain the theory of constraints
6. demonstrate the value of just-in-time manufacturing systems
7. describe the concept of cost of quality
8. calculate the cost savings resulting from reductions in inventories, reduction in production cycle time, production yield improvements, and reductions in rework and defect rates

SUMMARY

This chapter discusses the usefulness of identifying relevant costs and revenues for streamlining decision making across alternatives. The chapter explains why sunk costs are not relevant for economic decision making and discusses quantitative and qualitative factors that are important in outsourcing decisions. The choice of facility layout can streamline production operations and improve financial results. The theory of constraints, just-in-time systems, and cost of quality analyses can contribute toward more efficient operations and higher quality products and services.

REVIEW OF KEY TERMS AND CONCEPTS

> Learning Objective 1: Explain why sunk costs are not relevant costs.

I. Evaluation of Financial Implications

   A. Managers must evaluate the financial implications of decisions, and the appropriate trade-offs between costs and benefits resulting from different alternatives. The key question is: Which costs and revenues are relevant for decision making?

   B. **Relevant revenues and costs** are those that differ across decision alternatives; designation as relevant depends on the decision context and the alternatives available.

   C. **Sunk costs** are costs of resources that have already been committed, and, regardless of what decision managers make, these costs cannot be avoided. *Sunk costs are not considered relevant costs in evaluating alternatives.*

Carefully work through the Bonner Company example on relevant costs for the decision to purchase a new machine. Note that the purchase price of the old machine and the payments that must be made on it are sunk costs and not relevant for the decision. Further, **Exhibit 6-2** illustrates the relevant cash outflows and inflows.

> Learning Objective 2: Analyze make-or-buy decisions.

II. Make-or-Buy Decisions
   The **make-or-buy decision** is either to make a part or component in-house or purchase it from an outside supplier.

   A. **Outsourcing** is purchasing a product, part, or component from an outside supplier instead of manufacturing it in-house.

   B. **Avoidable costs** are those that are eliminated when a part, product, product line, or business segment is discontinued.

> Learning Objective 3: Demonstrate the influence of qualitative factors in making decisions.

C. **Qualitative factors**, such as permanence of an outside price or the reputation of a supplier, can influence decisions.

  1. Factors such as the supplier's ability to meet performance standards on time are critical to success. Some businesses have chosen to certify suppliers. A **certified supplier** is a specially selected supplier who is assured a high level of business for conforming to high standards for quality and delivery schedules.

  2. A company may choose to produce in-house all components that use critical technologies so it can retain its leadership and control over innovations in important areas.

 Exhibit 6-3 provides examples of make-or-buy comparisons.

Learning Objective 4: Compare the different types of facilities layouts.

Learning Objective 5: Explain the theory of constraints.

III. Facility Layout Systems

  A. The **theory of constraints** (TOC) maintains that operating income can be increased by carefully managing the bottlenecks in a process. A bottleneck is any condition that impedes or constrains the efficient flow of a process.

  1. The TOC relies on three measures.

    a. **Throughput contribution** is the difference between revenues and direct materials for the quantity of product sold.

    b. **Investment** is the monetary value of the assets that the organization gives up to acquire an asset.

    c. **Operating costs** are all other costs, except for direct materials costs, that are needed to obtain throughput contribution. Examples: depreciation and utility costs.

  2. The TOC emphasizes the short-run optimization of throughput contribution.

 Because TOC proponents view operating costs as difficult to alter in the short run, ABC-type analyses of activities and cost drivers are not conducted. See, however, the "In Practice" box entitled "ABC versus TOC: Will Ever the Twain Meet?"

        3.   The TOC can guide the process of streamlining operations, regardless of the type of facility design.

   B.   **Facility layout systems** can affect cycle time of production, as well as the level of inventories and inventory-related costs.

        1.   **Process layout** is a means of organizing a production activity so that all similar equipment or functions are grouped together. For example, in most printing shops, similar machines are grouped together. Process layouts often:

            a.   Exist where production occurs in small batches of unique products

            b.   Lead to long production paths and high work-in-process inventory levels

        2.   **Product layout** is a means of organizing a production activity so that equipment or functions are organized to make a specific product. An automobile assembly line is an example of a product layout.

        3.   **Cellular manufacturing** is a way of organizing the plant into a number of cells so that within each cell, all machines required to manufacture a group of similar products are arranged sequentially in close proximity to each other.

Exhibit 6-4 illustrates the system that newspaper publisher Gannet Corporation uses. The system has reduced cycle time and costs by eliminating the physical movement of work in process. **Exhibit 6-5** depicts the common U-shaped cell layout.

IV.   Inventory Costs and Processing Time

   A.   Batch production creates inventory costs and delays associated with storing and moving inventory. Batch processing may create delays in service industries, as well. Example: bank loan processing.

   B.   Inventory-related costs include the cost of moving, handling, and storing work in process, as well as costs of obsolescence or damage.

   C.   Manufacturing **cycle time** is the total time required to produce a product from start to finish, beginning from the receipt of raw materials from the supplier to the delivery of the finished goods to the distributors and customers. Therefore, storage time in a finished goods warehouse is considered part of manufacturing cycle time. Times devoted to four types of activities are summed together give total cycle time:

1. Processing

2. Moving

3. Storing (waiting)

4. Inspecting

D. **Manufacturing cycle efficiency (MCE)**, a widely used measure for assessing process efficiency, is the ratio of the actual processing time to total cycle time.

$$MCE = \frac{\text{Processing time}}{\text{Processing time} + \text{Moving time} + \text{Storage time} + \text{Inspection time}}$$

Carefully work through **Exhibits 6-6 through 6-10** on San RafaelElectric Corporation. In Exhibit 6-10, note the cost savings from reducing the financing investment in work-in-process inventory. Study the dialogue between Mike Richardson (plant controller) and the production and sales managers. Interviews of this sort are extremely important to gather the necessary information to make informed decisions.

E. New manufacturing practices can improve profitability by:

1. Reducing inventory-related financing

2. Reducing the demand placed on many support activity resources

3. Increasing sales through decreases in cycle time

Learning Objective 7: Describe the concept of cost of quality.

V. Cost of Nonconformance and Quality Issues

A. The **cost of nonconformance (CONC) to quality standards** is the cost incurred by an organization if products and services do not conform to quality standards.

B. Quality can be viewed as determined by two major factors:

1. Satisfying customer expectations regarding the attributes and performance of a product, such as its functionality and features

Management Accounting Information for Activity and Process Decisions **85**

2. Ensuring that the technical aspects of the product's design and performance conform to the manufacturer's standards

C. The ISO 9000 Standards, developed in Europe in 1987, provide globally recognized quality standards for products and services. Exhibit 6-11 provides details on the ISO guidelines, consisting of five standards.

D. In the United States, the American Quality Control Society has developed its own standards, Q90-Q94. Exhibit 6-12 discusses these in more detail.

E. Cost of Quality Categories

1. **Prevention costs** are incurred to ensure that companies produce products according to quality standards. Examples include quality engineering, training employees in methods to maintain quality, and statistical process control.

2. **Appraisal costs** typically are those related to inspecting products to ensure that they meet both internal and external customer requirements. Examples include inspection of incoming materials, process control monitoring, and product quality audits.

3. **Internal failure costs** occur when the manufacturing process produces a defective component or product and detects the failure internally. Examples include the cost of downtime in production as a result of discovering defectives and scrap and rework costs.

4. **External failure costs** are those incurred if a customer discovers a defective product or component once it has left the factory. Examples include warranty costs, service calls, product liability recalls, and product liability lawsuits.

Exhibit 6-13 provides examples of quality related costs in each of the four categories listed above.

F. A **cost-of-quality (COQ) report** details the cost of quality by the following categories: prevention, appraisal, internal failure, and external failure.

Learning Objective 6: Demonstrate the value of just-in-time manufacturing systems.

VI. Just-in-Time Manufacturing

   A. **Just-in-time (JIT) manufacturing** refers to making a good or providing a service only when the customer, who may be internal or external, requires it. Organizations that use JIT manufacturing must eliminate all sources of failure in the system. JIT manufacturing helps avoid many of the costs and service problems associated with conventional manufacturing and facilities layout.

   B. Management accounting:

   1. Must support the move to JIT by monitoring, identifying, and communicating to decision makers the sources of delay, error, and waste in the system

   2. Is simplified by JIT because there are fewer inventories to monitor and record

   C. JIT implementation requires managing a major cultural change for an organization.

Learning Objective 8: Calculate the cost savings resulting from reductions in inventories, reduction in production cycle time, production yield improvements, and reductions in rework and defect rates.

VII. Improvements in Production Yield
The Tobor Toy Company example illustrates a company's improvements, such as decreasing rework and reducing cycle time. Thomas Archer studied the following in analyzing the situation.

   A. Production flows (note the flowchart in Exhibit 6-14).

   B. Work-in-process inventory.

   C. Production costs (see Exhibit 6-15).

   D. Cost of rework. **Rework** consists of production activities required to bring defective units up to minimum quality standards (see Exhibit 6-16).

   E. Cost of carrying work-in-process inventory.

   F. Incremental production costs and contribution margin per robot (see Exhibit 6-17).

   G. Summary of benefits. Exhibit 6-18 summarizes the annual benefits from the JIT system.

Work through **Exhibits 6-14 to 6-18**. Understanding the process that Thomas Archer went through will provide you with insight into how quality improvements can be made.

 When reviewing this material, note the strong ties between management accounting and operations management. Throughout the textbook, other links related to strategy and organizational behavior are made.

PRACTICE TEST QUESTIONS AND PROBLEMS

True/False

_____ 1. In general, improvements in yield rate should improve production cycle time.

_____ 2. The costs and revenues that are relevant depend on the decision context and the alternatives available.

_____ 3. Although sunk costs are costs of resources that have been committed, they can still be influenced by the manager.

_____ 4. When making a decision to purchase a new machine, the purchase price of the old machine is a relevant cost.

_____ 5. When making a decision to purchase a new machine, the disposal value of an old machine is a relevant cost.

_____ 6. In general, with respect to outsourcing decisions, facility-sustaining costs are avoidable costs.

_____ 7. The theory of constraints emphasizes the short-run optimization of throughput contribution.

_____ 8. Process layouts tend to be used in organizations in which production is done in small batches.

_____ 9. Production cycle time begins when raw materials are received and ends when the product is finished and sent to the finished goods warehouse.

_____ 10. One of the principal inventory-related costs is that of financing the funds tied up in inventory.

Multiple-Choice

1. Each of the following should result in reductions in the level of work-in-process inventory and cycle time, EXCEPT
    (a) quality improvement programs.
    (b) corporate downsizing programs.
    (c) just-in-time programs.
    (d) cellular manufacturing.

2. Which of the following is NOT one of the four cost of quality categories?
    (a) Appraisal costs
    (b) Internal failure costs
    (c) Prevention costs
    (d) Benchmarking costs

3. One behavioral factor that may cause managers to not replace a new machine when they should is
    (a) their reputation.
    (b) the poor salvage value of the old machine.
    (c) what to do with the old machine.
    (d) the cost of the new machine.

4. Each of the following should be considered in the make-or-buy decision, EXCEPT
    (a) unavoidable facility-sustaining costs.
    (b) the cost to produce the product.
    (c) the cost to purchase the product outside the firm.
    (d) the general implications for the firm to buy the product from another firm.

5. The cost of which of the following is an example of an appraisal cost in the cost of quality framework?
    (a) Maintenance of test equipment
    (b) Statistical process control
    (c) Supplier certification
    (d) Product liability recalls

6. Each of the following kinds of costs is incurred when implementing a cellular manufacturing layout, EXCEPT
    (a) the cost of moving machines.
    (b) the cost of new insurance for workers.
    (c) the costs of training the workers.
    (d) the cost of reinstallation of the machines.

7. The financial benefits of cellular manufacturing include all of the following, EXCEPT
    (a) reduction in the number of material handlers needed.
    (b) reduction in the cost of storage.
    (c) reduction in materials wastage.
    (d) reduction in depreciation of the plant.

8. Shields Company has capacity to produce 5000 units of product HI99. Currently it is producing 3900 units. Foster Company asks Shields to produce 800 more units of HI99 for a special order. Neither new machinery nor extra plant space is needed for the special order. Which of the following statements is true?
   (a) Only product-sustaining costs will increase.
   (b) Only facility-sustaining costs will increase.
   (c) Both product-sustaining and facility-sustaining costs will increase.
   (d) Neither product-sustaining nor facility-sustaining costs will increase.

9. As the amount of work-in-process decreases, we expect all of the following to occur, EXCEPT
   (a) the wage rate per worker decreases.
   (b) inventory-related transactions decrease.
   (c) the number of shop floor workers decreases.
   (d) material handling decreases.

10. All of the following statements about just-in-time (JIT) are true, EXCEPT:
    (a) JIT means making a good or service only when the customer requires it.
    (b) Strictly speaking, JIT is a set of tools.
    (c) JIT processing systems must be reliable.
    (d) JIT is an approach to improvement that is continuous.

Completion

1. The four types of activity times included in computing total cycle time are: _____, _____, _____, and _____.

2. The _____ __ _____ is the cost incurred by an organization if products and services do not conform to quality standards.

3. The four-category quality cost framework results from experience that shows it is much less expensive to _____ defects than to _____ and _____ them after they have occurred.

4. _____ means buying products from an outside supplier instead of making them in-house.

5. _____ costs are those eliminated when a product is discontinued.

6. Manufacturing cycle efficiency is the ratio of _____ time to total _____ _____.

7. When all machines required for the manufacture of a group of similar products are arranged sequentially in close proximity to each other, we refer to this as _____ _____.

8. In _____-__-_____ production, no work-in-process inventories are required between the various stages of operations.

9. Two potential benefits of plant reorganization are increased _____ and reduced _____-_____ costs.

10. _____ consists of production activities required to bring defective units up to minimum quality standards.

Problems

1. Olafson Company is determining whether to outsource product L15. An outside bidder has quoted a price of $52. The following costs of the product when produced in-house are shown below and expressed on a per-unit basis.

Direct materials	$13.95
Direct labor	$15.00
Unit-related overhead	$17.80
Batch-related overhead	$6.55
Product-sustaining overhead	$3.25
Facility-sustaining overhead	$8.35
	$64.90

    (a) What assumptions need to be made about the behavior of support (overhead) costs?

    (b) Should Olafson Company outsource the product?

2. Eastco purchased a stamping machine four months ago and now realizes that a much better machine is available on the market. The following information pertains to both machines.

	Old Machine	New Machine
Acquisition cost	$150,000	$200,000
Remaining life	3 years	3 years
Current disposal value	$ 60,000	—
Salvage value at the *end of 3 years*	$ 6,000	$ 9,000

Annual operating costs for the old machine are $60,000 and the new machine will reduce annual operating costs by $48,000. These amounts do not include any charges for depreciation. Eastco uses the straight-line method of depreciation. The estimates above also do not include rework costs. The new stamping machine also will reduce the defect rate from 4% to 2%. All defective units are reworked at a cost of $1.25 per unit. Eastco produces 150,000 units annually.

(a) Should Eastco replace the old machine (ignore the time value of money)?

(b) What costs are considered sunk costs for this decision?

3. KWT Company prepared the following cost-of-quality report for last year, when sales were $25,000,000. Based on the report, what recommendations do you have for KWT Company?

	Annual Cost	Cost/Sales
Prevention Costs:		
Quality Engineering	$300,000	0.0120
Statistical Process Control	150,000	0.0060
Supplier Certification	10,000	0.0004
	$460,000	0.0184
Appraisal Costs:		
Inspection of Incoming Materials	$800,000	0.0320
Maintenance of Test Equipment	400,000	0.0160
Product Quality Audits	450,000	0.0180
Process Control Monitoring	1,000,000	0.0400
	$2,650,000	0.1060
Internal Failure Costs:		
Rework Costs	$600,000	0.0240
Net Cost of Scrap	200,000	0.0080
	$800,000	0.0320
External Failure Costs:		
Warranty Claims	$400,000	0.0160
Product Liability Recalls	500,000	0.0200
	$900,000	0.0360

SOLUTIONS TO PRACTICE TEST QUESTIONS AND PROBLEMS

True/False

1. True. In general, improvements in yield rate should improve production cycle time.

2. True. The costs and revenues that are relevant depend on the decision context and the alternatives available.

3. False. Sunk costs cannot be influenced by a manager.

4. False. When making a decision to purchase a new machine, the purchase price of the old machine is a sunk cost, not a relevant cost.

5. True. When making a decision to purchase a new machine, the disposal value of an old machine is a relevant cost.

6. False. With respect to outsourcing, facility-sustaining costs (for example, those relating to building and equipment) are usually unavoidable, especially in the short run.

7. True. The theory of constraints emphasizes the short-run optimization of throughput contribution, which is the difference between revenues and direct materials for the quantity of product sold.

8. True. Process layouts are used for production in small batches.

9. False. Production cycle time begins with the receipt of raw materials and ends with the delivery of finished goods to distributors and customers (not to the warehouse).

10. True. Financing the funds tied up in inventory is one of the most significant inventory-related costs.

Multiple-Choice

1. b. Corporate downsizing is unlikely to reduce work-in-process inventory and cycle time. In fact, it might increase both if the workforce is reduced significantly during downsizing.

2. d. The fourth category of costs is external failure costs.

3. a. Reputation is a critical variable for many managers. If they feel that replacing a new machine would convey that they made a mistake, they may try to save their reputation by not purchasing the new machine.

4. a. Unavoidable costs are not included in the make-or-buy decision, as they are irrelevant to the analysis.

5. a. The cost of maintenance of test equipment is an appraisal cost; costs of statistical process control and supplier certification are prevention costs; costs of product liability recalls are external failure costs.

6. b. New insurance is not needed when cellular manufacturing is implemented.

7. d. Reduction of depreciation expense of the plant is not a financial benefit of cellular manufacturing.

8. d. Because no new machinery or floor space is needed, neither product-sustaining nor facility-sustaining costs will increase.

9. a. The wage rate per worker will not decrease.

10. b. JIT is not just a set of tools. Instead, JIT is a philosophy of manufacturing that stresses quality and continuous improvement.

Completion

1. processing, moving, storing (waiting), inspecting

2. cost of nonconformance

3. prevent, detect, repair

4. Outsourcing

5. Avoidable

6. processing, cycle time

7. cellular manufacturing

8. just-in-time

9. sales (because of reduced cycle time), inventory-related

10. Rework

Problems

1. (a) Assumptions must be made about which overhead (support) costs are avoidable if Olafson outsources the product. Batch-related and product-sustaining support costs are most likely avoidable, but facility-sustaining support costs may be unavoidable if the plant cannot be converted to another use when L15 is outsourced.

    (b) Assuming that only facility-sustaining costs are unavoidable, the relevant costs per unit of producing L15 are:

Direct materials	$13.95
Direct labor	15.00
Unit-related overhead	17.80
Batch-related overhead	6.55
Product-sustaining overhead	3.25
Total	$56.55

    The difference in cost is $56.55 − $52 = $4.55. L15 should be outsourced unless some of the other overhead costs are unavoidable and total more than $4.55.

2. (a)

Net benefits over 3 years with the new machine	New Machine – Old Machine
Salvage value difference ($9,000 – $6,000)	$3,000
Decrease in annual operating costs (3 years × $48,000)	144,000
Reduction in rework costs (150,000 × 2% × $1.25 × 3 years)	11,250
Acquisition of new machine	(200,000)
Current disposal value of old machine	65,000
Net cash inflow	$18,250

Thus, Eastco should purchase the new machine.

(b) The acquisition cost of the old machine is a sunk cost.

3. Although KWT Company has a relatively low proportion of prevention, internal failure, and external failure costs, it has high proportion of appraisal costs. KWT should consider shifting some of the emphasis away from appraisal, to prevention. For example, inspection of incoming materials could be greatly reduced by a more aggressive program of supplier certification.

chapter 7

Cost Information for Pricing and Product Planning

Learning Objectives

After reading this chapter, you will be able to

1. show how a firm chooses its product mix in the short term.

2. explain the way a firm adjusts its prices in the short term depending on whether capacity is limited.

3. discuss how a firm determines a long-term benchmark price to guide its pricing strategy.

4. evaluate the long-term profitability of products and market segments.

SUMMARY

This chapter examines appropriate use of cost information in pricing and product-mix decisions. Analyses vary depending on whether the firm is a price taker or a price setter. The cost analyses also depend on the time frame involved in the decision. Other key ideas in this chapter include incremental costs, full costs, opportunity costs, and maximizing contribution per unit of scarce resource.

REVIEW OF KEY TERMS AND CONCEPTS

> Learning Objective 1: Show how a firm chooses its product mix in the short term.

I. Role of Product Costs in Pricing and Product Mix Decisions

   A. Understanding how product costs should be analyzed is extremely important for pricing decisions when a firm can set or influence the prices of its products.

   B. Product cost analysis is also important if prices are set by market forces. The firm can use product cost analysis in deciding the product mix to produce and sell.

   C. Firms may use product cost analysis in deciding how best to deploy marketing and promotion resources.

   D. Short-Term and Long-Term Pricing Considerations

      1. Many resources committed to activities are more than likely fixed in the short term because capacities cannot be easily altered. In the long term, managers have more flexibility in adjusting the capacities of activity resources to match demand for resources.

      2. In the short term, special attention must be paid to the time period over which capacity is committed to fill an order because the commitment may constrain the firm and not allow it to seek more profitable opportunities.

      3. If production is constrained by inadequate capacity, overtime or the use of subcontractors can help augment capacity in the short term.

   E. With respect to the ability to influence market prices, there are two general types of firms—price takers and price setters.

      1. A **price-taker** firm is one that has little or no influence on the industry supply-and-demand forces and, consequently, on the prices of its products.

      2. A **price-setter** firm is one that sets or bids the prices of its products because it enjoys a significant market share in its industry segment.

 This chapter discusses the four situations in **Exhibit 7-1**'s diagram. The situations include price-taker and price-setter firms, and short-term and long-term decisions.

II. Short-Term Product Mix Decisions—Price Takers

   A. Small firms who are price takers have little influence on the overall industry supply and demand and, thus, little influence on the prices of its undifferentiated products. Small firms cannot demand a higher price for their products without risking losing their customers to competitors. If a small firm tries to lower prices below industry prices, large firms might retaliate by engaging in a price war that would make the small firm and the industry worse off.

B. The simple decision rule for a price-taker firm is *to sell as many of its products as possible as long as their costs are less than their prices.* But two considerations must be kept in mind:

1. What costs are **relevant** to the short-term product mix decision? Should all product costs be included or only those that vary in the short term?

2. Managers may not be able to produce and sell more of those products whose costs are less than their prices given capacity constraints. In other words, how **flexible** are the capacities of the firm's activity resources?

Exhibits 7-2 through 7-7 on HKTex Company provide a comprehensive example of short-term product mix decisions. Work through this example carefully.

3. The HKTex example illustrates a key principle for short-term product mix decisions when prices are unaffected by the quantities sold. The criterion used to decide which products are the most profitable to produce and sell at prevailing prices is the **contribution (or contribution margin) per unit of the constrained resource** (which was machine hours in this example). The **contribution per unit** is the price per unit less variable costs per unit.

C. The Impact of Opportunity Costs
A variation in the HKTex problem is a situation in which a decision maker chooses one alternative over another. Thus, an opportunity cost arises.

1. An **opportunity cost** is the potential benefit sacrificed, when, in selecting one alternative, another alternative is given up. In the HKTex example, if the company accepts the order of 2,000 shirts from the new customer (the selected alternative), then HKTex must give up production of some garments it is currently producing and selling. The opportunity cost in this case is the lost profit on the garments that can no longer be made and sold.

2. In the HKTex example, if the company accepts the new order, it should sacrifice production of the garment(s) with the **lowest contribution per unit of the constrained resource**. HKTex's price per unit of the new order should result in at least as much contribution margin per machine hour as HKTex must sacrifice from lost sales of current garments.

Cost Information for Pricing and Product Planning **99**

> Learning Objective 2: Explain how a firm adjusts its prices in the short term depending on whether capacity is limited.

III. Short-Term Pricing Decisions—Price Setters

   A. The **full costs** for a job are the sum of all costs (direct materials, direct labor, and support activity costs) assigned to the job.

   B. **Cost-plus pricing** is a pricing approach in which the price of a product is set by a markup percentage above cost.

   C. The **markup percentage** is determined by a company's desired profit margin and overall rate of return. (Recall from Chapter 4 that the **markup rate** is the ratio of the markup amount to the estimated costs for a job.)

   D. This section discusses the relationship between costs and prices bid by a supplier for special orders that do not involve long-term relationships with the customer. Two cases are discussed—available surplus capacity and no available surplus capacity.

The Tudor Rose Tools and Dies Company example in **Exhibit 7-8** illustrates developing a bid price based on full costs for a job.

   1. Available Surplus Capacity

      a. **Incremental costs** (or revenues) are the amount by which costs (or revenues) increase if one particular alternative is chosen instead of another. The **incremental cost per unit** is the amount by which the total costs of production and sales increase when one additional unit of that product is produced and sold.

      b. When sufficient capacity is available, the minimum acceptable price must at least cover the incremental costs to produce and deliver the order. Briefly, incremental revenues must be greater than incremental costs.

   2. No Available Surplus Capacity

      a. When there is no available capacity, a firm will have to incur costs to acquire the necessary capacity. This may mean operating the plant on an overtime basis.

      b. Again, the decision rule is that incremental revenues must be greater than incremental costs. In this case, however, incremental costs will be higher than when surplus capacity is available.

E. Relevant costs (or revenues) are the costs (or revenues) that differ across alternatives, and, therefore, must be considered in deciding which alternative is the best. Incremental costs are the relevant costs for the kinds of short-term decisions discussed above.

Learning Objective 3: Discuss how a firm determines a long-term benchmark price to guide its pricing strategy.

IV. Long-Term Pricing Decisions—Price Setters

   A. Relevant costs for short-term special-order pricing decisions differ from full costs. What is the benefit of having full cost information?

   B. Reliance on full costs for pricing can be economically justified in three types of situations:

      1. Development and production of customized products

      2. Government contracts and pricing in regulated industries (such as electric utilities) that specify prices as full costs with a markup

      3. Over the long term, managers have greater flexibility in adjusting the level of commitment for all activity resources. Thus, full costs are relevant for long-term pricing decisions

   C. Because of short-term fluctuations in the demand for products, firms adjust their prices up and down over a period of time. Over the long term, their average prices tend to equal the price based on full costs that may be set in a long-term contract.

   D. The amount of markup is contingent on several factors:

      1. If the **strength of demand** for the product is high, a higher markup may be used.

      2. **Demand is elastic** if a small increase in price results in a large decrease in demand. Markups are lower when demand is elastic.

      3. When **competition is intense**, markups decrease, because it is hard for firms to sustain prices much higher than their incremental costs.

      4. Markups may be purposefully lowered based on firm strategy. Two types of strategies are:

         a. A **penetration pricing strategy**, which is charging a lower price initially to win market share from an established product of a competing firm

b. A **skimming price strategy**, which involves charging a higher price initially from customers willing to pay more for the privilege of possessing a new product

---

Learning Objective 4: Evaluate the long-term profitability of products and market segments.

V. Long-Term Product Mix Decisions—Price Takers

  A. Decisions to add new, or drop existing, products from the product portfolio often have long-term implications for the cost structure of the firm.

  B. Resources committed for batch-related and product- sustaining activities cannot be easily changed in the short term, so the mix cannot be changed quickly.

  C. In some cases, customers may desire a firm to maintain a full product line so that they do not have to go elsewhere. Thus, some unprofitable products may have to be kept to maintain the entire product line. If this is too costly, managers might try methods such as reengineering to lower the cost of some products.

  D. One caveat is that dropping products will help profitability only if managers also eliminate, or redeploy, the activity resources no longer required to support the dropped product.

The summary example on **Faxtronics** reviews the concepts of maximizing contribution per unit of scarce resource, special orders, and opportunity cost in relation to product mix decisions.

VI. Economic Analysis of the Pricing Decision (Appendix 7-1)

  A. The objective of the Appendix is to present an economic analysis of the pricing decision. Note that knowledge of basic differential calculus is needed to work through the examples.

  B. The quantity choice is examined and presented in terms of equating marginal revenue and marginal cost. **Marginal revenue** (or cost) is the increase in revenue (or cost) corresponding to a unit increase in the quantity produced and sold.

Carefully work through the analysis and study the graph in **Exhibit 7-10**.

PRACTICE TEST QUESTIONS AND PROBLEMS

True/False

_____ 1. An important function of a cost management system is to supply cost information so that managers can make product pricing and mix decisions.

_____ 2. In the short term, managers have a great deal of flexibility in adjusting the capacities of resources to match the demand for these resources.

_____ 3. Firms in industries in which products are highly customized are often price setters.

_____ 4. The key criterion to use in short-term product mix decisions when deciding which products are the most profitable to produce and sell at current prices is the contribution per unit of constrained resource.

_____ 5. Full costs can never be used for pricing.

_____ 6. The elasticity of demand has a direct effect on markups.

_____ 7. A penetration pricing strategy involves a firm choosing to use a low markup for a new product.

_____ 8. Resources committed for product-sustaining activities can be easily changed in the short term.

_____ 9. A firm may choose to keep an unprofitable product in order to offer a full product line.

_____ 10. Dropping products will always improve profitability.

Multiple-Choice

1. Short-term pricing decisions depend on all of the following, EXCEPT
   (a) whether surplus capacity is available for additional production.
   (b) whether the available capacity limits production.
   (c) the time period of the contract over which capacity is committed.
   (d) the level of product-sustaining activities and costs.

2. A small firm on the fringe of an industry is probably
   (a) a price setter.
   (b) a price taker.
   (c) both a price taker and a price setter.
   (d) a price maker.

3. Cherilee Company produces two products, AR4 and AR8. AR4 has a contribution per unit of $3.00 and requires .3 machine hours per unit, whereas AR8 has a contribution of $2.50 and requires .2 machine hours per unit. The company's policy is to sell only products with a contribution per machine hour, the constrained resource, greater than $9.90. What should they do?
   (a) Sell both AR4 and AR8.
   (b) Sell only AR4.
   (c) Sell only AR8.
   (d) Sell neither AR4 nor AR8.

4. An opportunity cost is
   (a) completely intangible and not measurable.
   (b) the sacrificed potential benefit of choosing one alternative over another.
   (c) the sacrificed past benefit of choosing one alternative over another.
   (d) not relevant to any decision.

5. Lido Company manufactures product MY40. Currently, the product sells for $55, with total costs to manufacture equaling $30. In order to add a new feature to the product, additional direct materials of $3.00, direct labor of $2.50, and batch-related costs of $1.45 per unit would have to be incurred. What are the incremental costs per unit of the decision to add the new feature?
   (a) $3.00
   (b) $2.50
   (c) $6.95
   (d) $5.50

6. Full-cost pricing is LEAST likely to be economically justified under which of the following?
   (a) When customized products are produced
   (b) When contracts are developed with governmental agencies
   (c) When a firm enters into a long-term contractual relationship with a customer to supply a product
   (d) When a firm enters into a short-term contractual relationship with a customer to supply a product

7. Markups are least affected by
   (a) sudden changes in technology.
   (b) elasticity of demand.
   (c) intensity of competition.
   (d) strength of demand.

8. Demand is elastic when
   (a) a small increase in price results in a small decrease in demand.
   (b) price increases cause demand to fluctuate wildly.
   (c) a small increase in price results in a large decrease in demand.
   (d) price increases cause demand to increase.

9. Which of the following strategies to reduce the cost of a product is the least effective?
   (a) Reengineer the product.
   (b) Reduce the number of features of the product.
   (c) Offer customers incentives to increase order sizes.
   (d) Improve production processes to reduce setup time.

10. For long-term product mix decisions, comparison of the price of a product with its _____ costs provides a valuable evaluation of its long-term profitability.
    (a) variable
    (b) opportunity
    (c) incremental
    (d) activity-based

Completion

1. Even when prices are set by overall market supply-and-demand forces and the firm has little influence on product prices, managers use cost information to decide the ____ of products to _____ and ____ given their market prices.

2. Decisions to introduce new products or eliminate existing ones have ____-____ consequences, and our emphasis in analyzing such decisions is on the demand each product places on _____ _____.

3. A small firm, or a firm with a negligible market share, behaves as a _____ _____.

4. The contribution margin, or contribution from each of the firm's products to the firm's profits, is determined by subtracting the _____ _____ from the price of the product.

5. Giving up the production of a profitable product for another results in an _____ cost.

6. The _____ costs of a product are the sum of direct materials, direct labor, and support costs.

7. _____ costs are defined as the amount by which costs increase if one particular decision is made instead of another.

8. _____ costs are defined as the costs that must be considered in deciding which alternative is best.

9. A supplier bidding on special orders that do not involve long-term relationships with the customer should compare _____ _____ to _____ _____.

10. When a _____ pricing strategy is used, a higher price is charged to customers willing to pay for the privilege of possessing the latest technological innovations.

Problems

1. Plasticraft Company produces and sells a single product called a DROID. Plasticraft has excess capacity to manufacture 5,000 additional DROIDS. Variable costs are $35 per unit, and fixed costs total $300,000 per month. Ajax Company has offered to pay Plasticraft $39 per unit for a one-time special order for 4,000 DROIDS. This special order requires some additional selling expenses of $1.50 per unit. Should Plasticraft accept this special order?

2. Superior Company produces two porcelain figurines of Lucy and Linus. The selling prices and variable costs for each figurine are as follows:

	Linus	Lucy
Selling price	$25.00	$20.00
Variable costs:		
Direct materials	9.00	6.00
Direct labor	5.00	2.00
Support	4.00	2.00

   The cost of direct labor is $10.00 per hour and only 500 hours of labor time are available each week.

   (a) Determine the contribution margin per direct labor hour for each product.

(b) Which product should Superior's sales force promote?

SOLUTIONS TO PRACTICE TEST QUESTIONS AND PROBLEMS

True/False

1. True. This is a critical function of cost management systems.

2. False. In the short term, managers have little flexibility in adjusting the capacities of resources.

3. True. Such firms are often price setters.

4. True. The contribution per unit of constrained resource is the key concept.

5. False. There are a number of instances in which full costs can be used, such as government contracting.

6. True. The elasticity of demand has a direct effect on markups.

7. True. This is the definition of a penetration strategy.

8. False. Resources committed for product-sustaining activities cannot easily be changed in the short term.

9. True. In the short term, the firm may feel compelled to offer a full line of products. If the cost of one particular product is so high that it is unreasonable to keep the product, the firm must think of ways to phase it out and substitute different products for the customer.

10. False. Improving profitability after dropping products often requires that managers eliminate or redeploy the activity resources no longer required to support the product.

Multiple-Choice

1. d. The level of product-sustaining activities and costs are more relevant for long-term decisions.

2. b. Such firms are usually price takers.

3. a. Both AR4 and AR8 have contributions per unit of constrained resource (machine hours) greater than $9.90: AR4's is $10.00 and AR8's is $12.50. Thus, both AR4 and AR8 should be sold.

4. b. An opportunity cost is the sacrificed potential benefit of choosing one alternative over another.

5. c. The incremental costs are the sum of the additional direct materials, direct labor, and batch-related costs, or $6.95.

6. d. Full-cost pricing is least likely to be justified when a firm enters into a short-term contractual relationship with a customer to supply a product.

7. a. Markups are least affected by sudden changes in technology.

8. c. Demand is elastic when small increases in price cause large decreases in demand.

9. b. The least-effective strategy is to reduce the number of features of the product. Although this may reduce costs, it could make the product less appealing to customers.

10. d. For long-term product mix decisions, activity-based costs provide a valuable evaluation of long-term profitability because they reflect the consumption of different activity resources for the manufacture and sale of different products.

Completion

1. mix, manufacture, sell

2. long-term, activity resources

3. price taker

4. variable costs

5. opportunity

6. full

7. Incremental

8. Relevant

9. incremental revenue, incremental cost

10. skimming

Problems

1. Yes, Plasticraft should accept Ajax Company's offer, because it will increase its operating income by $10,000 = [$39 − ($35 + $1.50)] × 4,000 DROIDS.

2. (a) Contribution margin per direct labor hour for each product:

	Linus	Lucy
Selling price	$25.00	$20.00
Less:		
Variable costs		
Direct materials	9.00	6.00
Direct labor	5.00	2.00
Support	4.00	2.00
Contribution margin per figurine	$7.00	$10.00
Direct labor hours per figurine	0.5	0.2
Contribution margin per direct labor hour	$14.00	$50.00

(b) Superior's sales force should promote the Lucy figurine, because it has the higher contribution margin per unit of constrained resource (direct labor hours).

chapter 8

Capital Budgeting

ℒearning 𝒪bjectives

After reading this chapter, you will be able to

1. recognize the nature and importance of long-term (capital) assets.

2. understand why organizations control long-lived assets and short-term assets differently.

3. use the basic tools and concepts of financial analysis: investment, return on investment, future value, present value, annuities, and required rate of return.

4. use capital budgeting to evaluate investment proposals and recognize how the concepts of payback, accounting rate of return, net present value, internal rate of return, and economic value added relate to capital budgeting.

5. evaluate the effect of income taxes on investment decisions and show how to incorporate tax considerations in capital budgeting.

6. use what-if and sensitivity analyses in capital budgeting.

7. recognize how to include strategic considerations in capital budgeting.

8. use post-implementation audits in capital budgeting.

SUMMARY

This chapter discusses basic capital budgeting, which compares the costs and benefits of a long-term (capital) asset. The concept of present value is used to convert cash inflows and outflows to a common point in time so they are comparable. The concepts of payback period, accounting rate of return, internal rate of return, and economic value added are discussed in relation to capital budgeting. Planners can use what-if and sensitivity analyses to investigate the effects of estimation uncertainty. Subsequently, planners can conduct post-implementation audits to reassess the purchase of the asset.

REVIEW OF KEY TERMS AND CONCEPTS

> Learning Objective 1: Recognize the nature and importance of long-term (capital) assets.

> Learning Objective 2: Understand why organizations control long-lived assets and short-term assets differently.

I. The Importance of Long-Term (Capital) Assets
   The focus in this chapter is on investments in long-term assets. Long-term assets create the committed costs that we have labeled batch-related, product- and process-related and facility-sustaining.

   A. **Long-term (capital) assets** are equipment, facilities, or other assets that provide productive services to the organization for more than one year.

   B. The acquisition of long-term assets is important because:

      1. Organizations commit to long-term assets for extended periods of time, creating the potential for excess costs through excess capacity or lost opportunities through scarce capacity.

      2. The amount of capital committed is usually very large.

      3. The long-term nature of capital assets creates technological risk for organizations.

   C. **Capital budgeting** is a systematic approach to evaluating an investment in a long-term asset. The fundamental comparison is between future benefits and initial cost.

> Learning Objective 3: Use the basic tools and concepts of financial analysis: investment, return on investment, future value, present value, annuities, and required rate of return.

II. Basic Tools and Concepts of Financial Analysis

   A. **Investment** is the monetary value of the assets that the organization gives up to acquire a long-term asset.

B. **Return** is the increased cash flows in the future attributable to the long-term asset.

C. Investment and return are the foundations of capital budgeting analysis because the fundamental evaluation issue in dealing with a long-term asset is whether its future benefits justify its initial cost (the initial investment).

D. The **time value of money** is the concept that, because money can be invested to earn a return, the value of money depends on when it is received. Consequently, amounts of money received at different periods of time must be converted to their value at a common date to be compared.

E. Notation

    n **Number of periods** considered in the investment analysis; common period lengths are a month, a quarter, or a year.

    FV **Future value**, or ending value, of the investment n periods from now

    PV **Present value**, or value at the current moment in time, of an amount to be received n periods from now

    a **Annuity**, or equal amount, received or paid at the end of each period for n periods

    r **Rate of return** required, or expected, from an investment opportunity; the rate of interest earned on an investment

F. **Future value** is the amount to which a sum invested today will accumulate over a stated number of periods at a stated rate of return.

    1. One Period

        Future value of an investment in after one period = Investment × (1 + Periodic rate of return)

$$FV = PV \times (1 + r)$$

    2. Multiple Periods

        a. **Compounding effect (of interest)** is the phenomenon of earning interest on interest that was previously earned over multiple periods (see Exhibit 8-1).

        b. Future value of an investment in n periods = Investment $\times (1+r)^n$

$$FV = PV \times (1+r)^n$$

c. The formula above assumes that any return earned is not withdrawn until the end of n periods, and the rate of return is constant for the n periods.

The textbook illustrates computing future values in three ways: using a calculator, a future-value table (using **Exhibit 8-2**), or a computer spreadsheet program. **Exhibit 8-3** shows the path of compound growth for various rates of interest.

G. Present Value

1. **Present value** is the current monetary worth of an amount to be paid in the future under stated conditions of rate of return and compounding.

$$\text{Present value} = \frac{\text{Future amount received in period } n}{(1 + \text{Required periodic return})^n}$$

$$PV = \frac{FV}{(1+r)^n}$$

$$PV = FV \times (1+r)^n$$

2. **Inflows** are the incremental cash inflows associated with an asset.

3. **Outflows** are the incremental cash outflows associated with an asset.

4. **Time zero (or period zero)** is the point of time when the investment is undertaken.

5. **Discounting** is the process of computing present value.

The textbook illustrates computing present values in three ways: using a calculator, a present-value table (using **Exhibit 8-4**), or a computer spreadsheet program. **Exhibit 8-5** illustrates the decay in present value as the interest rate increases and the time period lengthens.

H. Present Value and Future Value of Annuities

1. An **annuity** is a contract that promises to pay a fixed amount each period for a stated number of periods.

The textbook describes how to compute the present value of an annuity using a calculator (see **Exhibit 8-6**), a present-value table (see **Exhibit 8-7**), or a computer spreadsheet program. The formula below (see Appendix 8-1) can also be used.

2. **Present value of an annuity**:

$$PV = a \times \left[\frac{(1+r)^n - 1}{r \times (1+r)^n}\right]$$

3. **Annuity required to repay a loan**: Present value concepts can be applied to compute the annuity required to repay a present value. A computer spreadsheet program or the following formula (see Appendix 8-1) can be used:

$$a = PV \times \left[\frac{r \times (1+r)^n}{(1+r)^n - 1}\right]$$

I. Cost of Capital

1. The **cost of capital**, also known as the risk-adjusted discount rate, is the return that the organization must earn on its investments in order to meet its investors' return requirements. The cost of capital is the benchmark an organization uses to evaluate investment proposals.

2. The cost of capital reflects the amount and cost of debt and equity in an organization's financial structure and the financial market's perception of the financial risk of the organization's activities.

3. The most widely used approach to computing the cost of capital for evaluating new investments is the **weighted average cost of capital**, illustrated in Exhibit 8-10.

> Learning Objective 4: Use capital budgeting to evaluate investment proposals and recognize how the concepts of payback, accounting rate of return, net present value, internal rate of return, and economic value added relate to capital budgeting.

III. Alternative Approaches to Capital Budgeting

Calculations for these approaches are illustrated in the Shirley's Doughnut Hole example. **Exhibit 8-11** illustrates the payback criterion. **Exhibit 8-12** provides a time line of cash flows, and **Exhibit 8-13** illustrates net present value calculations. **Exhibit 8-14** shows internal rate of return calculations.

A. The **payback period** is the number of periods required for the cash inflows associated with a project to recover the initial investment. The payback period approach ignores the time value of money and ignores cash flows that occur beyond the payback period. Nevertheless, the payback period approach is widely used in practice.

B. The **accounting rate of return** is average accounting income divided by average investment (the average of historical cost plus salvage value). Firms may view an investment as acceptable if the accounting rate of return for the investment is greater than a target rate of return. The accounting rate of return approach ignores the time value of money but considers cash flows in all periods.

C. Net Present Value

   1. **Net present value** is the sum of the present values of all the cash inflows and cash outflows associated with a project. Net present value explicitly incorporates the time value of money and considers cash flows in all periods.

   2. The following steps are used to compute an investment's net present value:

       Step 1. Choose the period length (for example, annual, quarterly, or semiannual lengths) to evaluate the investment proposal. The period length depends on the periodicity of the investment's cash flows.

       Step 2. Identify the organization's cost of capital, and convert it to an appropriate rate of return for the period length chosen in step 1.

       Step 3. Identify the incremental cash flows in each period of the project's life,

       Step 4. Use the organization's cost of capital to compute the present value of each period's cash flows.

       Step 5. Sum the present values of the cash inflows and outflows to determine the project's net present value.

       Step 6. If the project's net present value is positive, the project is acceptable from an economic perspective.

D. **Internal rate of return (IRR)** is the rate of return expected from an investment. Equivalently, IRR is the discount rate that makes a project's net present value equal zero. The internal rate of return approach is common in practice despite the following disadvantages:

   1. It assumes an organization can reinvest a project's intermediate cash flows at the project's IRR.

   2. It can create ambiguous results in some situations.

E. The **profitability index** is a variation on the net present value method, computed by dividing the present value of the cash inflows by the present value of the cash outflows. The profitability index is used to compare mutually exclusive projects of different sizes. Computation of profitability indexes is illustrated in Exhibit 8-16.

Exhibit 8-15 presents the results of a survey on organizations' investment justifications. Note that although the net present value approach is superior to the payback, IRR, and accounting rate of return approaches, all these methods are found in practice.

    F.   **Economic value added** is the organization's income according to generally accepted accounting principles (GAAP), adjusted to reverse biases introduced by the conservative nature of GAAP, minus the organization's cost of capital multiplied by the investment in the organization. In contrast to net present value analysis, the economic value added approach begins with accounting income rather than net cash flow. Consequently, economic value added is more suited to evaluating an ongoing investment than a new investment opportunity.

Learning Objective 5: Evaluate the effect of income taxes on investment decisions and show how to incorporate tax considerations in capital budgeting.

IV.   The Effect of Taxes on the Capital Budgeting Decision

    A.   The organization must pay taxes on net benefits (taxable income) provided by an investment.

    B.   Taxable income is defined by the tax jurisdiction and includes, among other things, a specification of how the organization may depreciate capital assets for tax purposes. Depreciation acts as a tax shield in that it offsets some of the taxes that would be paid. Gains on sales of assets are taxable; losses on sales of assets may offset taxable income, providing a tax shield. Exhibit 8-18 displays after-tax cash flows for the Shirley's Doughnut Hole example.

 Carefully work through the capital budgeting summary example along with **Exhibits 8-19 through 8-21**.

Learning Objective 6: Use what-if and sensitivity analyses in capital budgeting.

V.   Uncertainty in Cash Flows

    A.   Planners may deal with uncertainty in cash flows by estimating a probability distribution or by specifying a small set of possible outcomes and assigning probabilities that sum to one, as in Exhibit 8-22.

    B.   **What-if analysis** uses a model to predict the effect on outcomes of varying a model's key parameters or estimates.

C. **Sensitivity analysis** involves selectively varying key estimates of a plan or budget. Sensitivity analysis includes an investigation of the effect of a change in a parameter on a decision, rather than on an outcome.

Exhibit 8-23 shows that the annual expected cash flows must fall below $17,556 before Shirley's project becomes economically undesirable. **Exhibit 8-24** provides an example of dealing with uncertainty by assessing a probability distribution over the length of time a consultant will stay with a company.

Learning Objective 7: Recognize how to include strategic considerations in capital budgeting.

VI. Strategic benefits are important considerations in capital budgeting. To be recognized in capital budgeting analysis, the benefits must be expressed in dollar terms. Long-term assets can provide the following key strategic benefits:

A. Producing a product or providing a service that competitors cannot

B. Improving product quality by reducing the potential to make mistakes

C. Reducing the cycle time required to make a product

Learning Objective 8: Use post-implementation audits in capital budgeting.

VII. A **post-implementation audit** is a reassessment of a past decision to purchase a long-lived asset by comparing expected and actual inflows and outflows. The audit provides the following benefits:

A. By comparing estimates with results, planners can determine where their estimates were incorrect and try to avoid making the same mistakes in the future.

B. Rewards can be given to those who are good at making capital budgeting decisions.

C. A policy of conducting audits can help counter the temptation to inflate the benefits to get projects approved.

VIII. Appendix 8-1: Annuity Formulas

    A. Present Value of an Annuity

$$PV = a \times \left[\frac{(1+r)^n - 1}{r \times (1+r)^n} \right]$$

    B. Annuity to Repay a Loan

$$a = PV \times \left[\frac{r + (1+r)^n}{(1+r)^n - 1} \right]$$

IX. Appendix 8-2: Effective and Nominal Rates of Interest

    A. The **nominal rate of interest**, r_n, is the stated annual rate of interest.

    B. The **effective rate of interest**, r_e, is the actual annual rate of interest earned on an investment.

$$r_e = \left(1 + \frac{r_n}{n}\right)^n - 1$$

PRACTICE TEST QUESTIONS AND PROBLEMS

True/False

_____ 1. Long-term assets and capital assets refer to different concepts.

_____ 2. Under the payback method, a project is accepted if its payback period is greater than a critical value.

_____ 3. The time value of money applies only to investments over four years.

_____ 4. *Future value* refers to the value at the current moment in time of an amount to be received in the future.

_____ 5. A project's profitability index is computed by dividing the present value of the cash inflows by the present value of the cash outflows.

_____ 6. The process of computing present value is called compounding.

_____ 7. The accounting rate of return approach to capital budgeting ignores the time value of money.

_____ 8. The cost of capital reflects the amount and cost of debt and equity in a firm's financial structure.

_____ 9. The formula to compute future value n periods from time zero assumes that any interest earned is not withdrawn until the end of the n periods.

_____ 10. Depreciation of a capital investment can offset some of the taxes an organization would otherwise pay.

Multiple-Choice

1. All of the following are true about the payback period approach, EXCEPT that
    (a) it is widely used in practice.
    (b) it ignores cash flows that occur beyond the payback period.
    (c) it incorporates the time value of money.
    (d) it is the number of years taken for cash inflows associated with a project to recover the initial investment.

2. The future value of $1 10 years from now at an interest rate of 4% equals
    (a) $1.05.
    (b) $1.46.
    (c) $1.48.
    (d) $1.04.

3. Barney's Bread Shop has purchased equipment at a cost of $80,000. The expected life of the equipment is five years, and the expected salvage value at the end of five years is $10,000. For computing the accounting rate of return, the average investment is
    (a) $18,000.
    (b) $35,000.
    (c) $14,000.
    (d) $45,000.

4. Mitch and Doreen Shim want to accumulate $100,000 for their newborn child's education over the next 18 years. How much money at a 6% interest rate do they have to invest now to accumulate the $100,000?
    (a) $35,034.38
    (b) $ 9,235.65
    (c) $23,089.13
    (d) $37,043.15

5. The cost of capital is
    (a) the maximum return an organization must earn on its investments in order to meet its investors' return requirements.
    (b) the minimum return an organization must earn on its investments in order to meet its investors' return requirements.
    (c) the minimum return an organization must earn on its investments that last over 5 years.
    (d) the minimum return an organization must earn on its investments that last over 10 years.

6. The following are all important to calculating net present value of a new investment, EXCEPT
    (a) knowing the initial purchase price of previous capital assets.
    (b) determining the appropriate period length of the investment.
    (c) identifying the firm's cost of capital.
    (d) computing the present value of each period's cash flow.

7. Internal rate of return is
   (a) the minimum return an organization must earn on its investments in order to meet its investors' return requirements.
   (b) the minimum rate of return an organization chooses as its target.
   (c) the actual rate of return expected from an investment.
   (d) always equal to the net present value of a project.

8. Altadena Printing has just acquired a new machine for $70,000. It has a useful life of five years and salvage value of $7,500. If the company uses straight-line depreciation, how much depreciation can Altadena Printing claim each year?
   (a) $14,000
   (b) $15,500
   (c) $12,500
   (d) $13,000

9. Kamloops Lumber had taxable income of $825,000 in 2000. It also had depreciation expense of $150,000, and its income was taxed at the rate of 40%. What effect did tax reductions related to depreciation expense have on Kamloops Lumber's cash flow in 2000?
   (a) Increased cash flow by $150,000
   (b) Increased cash flow by $60,000
   (c) Increased cash flow by $90,000
   (d) Decreased cash flow by $60,000

10. Which of the following is not a benefit of performing post-implementation audits of capital budgeting decisions?
    (a) Planners can identify where their estimates were incorrect.
    (b) Planners will be more reluctant to inflate their estimates of benefits.
    (c) Planners will be encouraged to take on more risky investments.
    (d) Managers can identify and reward those who are good at making these types of decisions.

Completion

1. The long-term nature of capital assets can create _____ and _____ risk for organizations.

2. _____ _____ is a systematic approach to evaluating an investment in a long-term asset.

3. _____ _____ _____ _____ is average accounting income divided by average investment.

4. _____ _____ _____ is the sum of the present values of all the cash inflows and cash outflows associated with a project.

5. Because money has a time-dated value, a fundamental point to remember in capital budgeting is that in order to compare amounts of money received at different periods of time, the amounts must be converted to their _____ on a _____ date.

6. An __-_____ _____ is a contract that promises a constant amount each period over *n* periods.

7. _____ _____ _____ is an organization's GAAP income, adjusted for biases introduced by GAAP, minus the organization's cost of capital multiplied by the investment level.

8. When an amount of money is deposited in a bank and left to accumulate for multiple periods, the rate of growth is _____.

9. What-if analysis and sensitivity analysis are important in capital budgeting because of the uncertainties in _____ future cash flows.

10. Reviewing the decision to purchase a long-lived asset is called a _____-_____ _____.

Problems

1. You have just found out that you won the California State Lottery. The grand prize is $18,000,000. The prize is paid out so that you will receive $360,000 every half year for the next 25 years. What is the present value of the lottery prize if the current semi-annual rate of interest offered by a bank is 4%, compounded semiannually?

2. A government savings bond will pay the holder $750 in 20 years. If the bond market is now requiring 5% annual interest on government debt, what will be the present value of this bond?

3. Sarah Quinn wants to retire in 25 years with $5,000,000 in her bank. If she can invest funds to earn 12.5% compounded annually, what amount must she invest each year to accumulate $5,000,000 at the end of 25 years?

4. Bill and Shannon have decided to retire from their jobs in Ann Arbor, Michigan. They plan to construct an amusement park in Flint, Michigan. The amusement park building cost would be $1,000,000 per year for 2 years. The park would be open in year 3 and would generate $400,000 per year in net cash flows. Bill and Shannon have a required return of 15% on all of their investments.

The land on which the amusement park will be built is leased, and the lease cost is included in the annual net cash flow calculation. The lease will be terminated after 10 years, and thus the park will be able to operate for 8 years. Bill and Shannon will not be compensated in any way for the work done to build the park, and will simply walk away from it when the lease is up.

Compute the net present value of the decision to build the amusement park. Should Bill and Shannon make the investment? Ignore taxes in your analysis.

SOLUTIONS TO PRACTICE TEST QUESTIONS AND PROBLEMS

True/False

1. False. Long-term assets and capital assets refer to the same concepts.

2. False. Under the payback method, a project is accepted if its payback period is less than a critical value.

3. False. The time value of money concept can be applied for any period of time.

4. False. *Present value* refers to the value at the current moment in time, of an amount to be received in the future.

5. True. A project's profitability index is computed by dividing the present value of the cash inflows by the present value of the cash outflows. The profitability index approach is used to compare mutually exclusive projects with different sizes.

6. False. The process of computing present value is called discounting.

7. True. The accounting rate of return focuses on accounting income rather than on cash flows and the time value of money.

8. True. The cost of capital reflects the amount and cost of debt and equity in a firm's financial structure.

9. True. The formula also assumes the interest rate is constant for all *n* periods.

10. True. Organizations are allowed to depreciate a capital investment to offset some of the taxes they would otherwise pay.

Multiple-Choice

1. c. Although the payback period approach does not incorporate the time value of money or take into account cash flows beyond the payback period, it is widely used in practice.

2. c. The future value is $(1.04)^{10} = 1.48$.

3. d. The average investment is the average of the initial investment and the salvage value, or $(80,000 + 10,000)/2 = \$45,000$.

4. a. Present value $= [\$100,000/(1.06)^{10}] = \$35,034.38$.

5. b. The cost of capital is the minimum return an organization must earn on its investments in order to meet its investors' return requirements.

6. a. Knowing the initial purchase price of previous capital assets is not necessary when calculating net present value of a new investment.

7. c. Internal rate of return is the actual rate of return expected from an investment. In other words, it is the interest rate that produces a net present value of zero for an investment.

8. c. Depreciation expense for Altadena Printing is $(\$70,000 - \$7500)/5 = \$12,500$.

9. b. Taxes were $\$60,000 = 150,000 \times 40\%$ lower with the depreciation expense deducted from income. Therefore, the net cash flow was $60,000 higher.

10. c. Under post-implementation audits, the risk and return of each investment will be evaluated, but by no means will planners always be encouraged to take on more risky projects, as a rule.

Completion

1. financial, technological

2. Capital budgeting

3. Accounting rate of return

4. Net present value

5. value, common

6. n-period annuity

7. Economic value added

8. compounded (or exponential)

9. estimating

10. post-implementation audit

Problems

1. Using the formula for the present value of an annuity, the prize value is

$$\$360,000 \times \frac{(1+0.04)^{50} - 1}{0.04 \times (1+0.04)^{50}} = \$360,000 \times 21.482 = \$7,733,520.$$

2. The present value of the bond is

$$\$750 \times \frac{1}{(1.05)^{20}} = \$750 \times 0.377 = \$282.75.$$

3. This problem asks for the amount of yearly annuity payments to arrive at a *future value* of $5,000,000. The formula for an annuity to repay a loan given a *present value* can be modified for a *future value*:

$$a = \frac{FV}{(1+r)^n} \times \left[\frac{r \times (1+r)^n}{(1+r)^n - 1}\right] = FV \times \left[\frac{r}{(1+r)^n - 1}\right]$$

Sarah's annual payment required is therefore:

$$\$5,000,000 \times \frac{0.125}{(1.125)^{25} - 1} = \$5,000,000 \times \frac{0.125}{18.0026} = \$34,717.$$

4. The incremental cost of the project is $1,000,000 per year for 2 years. This initial investment creates an annuity of $400,000 per year for 8 years.

Present value of 2 years of cash outflows equals:

$$\$1,000,000 \times \frac{(1+0.15)^2 - 1}{0.15 \times (1+0.15)^2} = \$1,625,708.88$$

Present value of 8 years of inflows of $400,000 (below, the present value will be adjusted for the starting point):

$$\$400,000 \times \frac{(1+0.15)^8 - 1}{0.15 \times (1+0.15)^8} = \$1,794,928.60$$

To convert the value of the 8 years of inflows at the start of year 3, which is the same as at the end of year 2, to the present:

$$\text{Present value} = \$1,794,928.60 \times \frac{1}{(1+0.15)^2} = \$1,357,223.90$$

The present value of the outflows ($1,625,708.88) is greater than the present value of the inflows, $1,357,223.90. On a purely economic basis, the project should not be undertaken because its net present value is negative ($268,484.91).

chapter 9

Management Accounting and Control Systems for Strategic Purposes: Assessing Performance over the Entire Value Chain

Learning Objectives

After reading this chapter, you will be able to

1. apply the concept of control

2. identify the characteristics of well-designed management accounting and control systems (MACS)

3. describe the total life cycle costing approach to managing product costs over the value chain

4. explain target costing

5. explain Kaizen costing

6. identify environmental costing issues

7. apply the process of benchmarking the best practices of other organizations

SUMMARY

This chapter expands the previous chapters' discussions of cost management systems to the larger entity of central performance measurement system known as a management accounting and control system (MACS). This chapter focuses on technical considerations in designing a MACS, and the next chapter discusses behavioral considerations. The methods discussed in this chapter include the total life cycle product costing approach, target costing, Kaizen costing, environmental costing, and benchmarking.

REVIEW OF KEY TERMS AND CONCEPTS

> Learning Objective 1: Discuss the concept of control.

I. "Control" in Management Accounting and Control Systems

    A. **Control** refers to the set of procedures, tools, performance measures, and systems that organization members use to guide and motivate all employees to achieve organizational objectives. A system is **in control** if it is on a path to achieving its objectives. Otherwise, the system is **out of control**.

    B. The process of keeping an organization in control consists of five steps:

        1. **Plan**: Develop the organization's objectives, choose activities to accomplish the objectives, and select measures to assess how well objectives are met.

        2. **Execute**: Implement the plan.

        3. **Monitor**: Measure the system's current performance level.

        4. **Evaluate**: Compare the system's planned and actual performance in order to identify discrepancies and take corrective actions.

        5. **Correct**: Take appropriate corrective actions to return the system to an in-control state.

 Exhibit 9-1 illustrates the cycle of control.

> Learning Objective 2: Identify the characteristics of well-designed management accounting and control systems (MACS).

II. Behavioral Characteristics of Well-Designed Management and Control Systems

    A. Embedding the organization's ethical code into MACS design.

    B. Using a mix of short- and long-term qualitative and quantitative performance measures.

    C. Empowering employees to be involved in decision making and MACS design.

    D. Developing an appropriate incentive system to reward performance.

III. Technical Considerations in Well-Designed Management and Control Systems

    A. **Relevance of information** refers to how useful information is for an organization's decision and control processes. The information must be:

        1. Accurate

        2. Timely

        3. Consistent (the language used and the technical methods of producing management accounting information should not conflict within various parts of an organization.)

        4. Flexible (permits customized applications for local decisions)

    B. The **scope** of a MACS includes the organization's entire value chain. The value chain:

        1. Is a sequence of activities that should contribute more to the ultimate value of the product than to its cost

        2. Begins with research, development, and engineering, moves through manufacturing, and continues on to customers

---

Learning Objective 3: Describe the total life cycle costing approach to managing product costs over the value chain.

IV. Total-Life-Cycle Product Costing (TLCC): The process of managing all costs along the value chain (managing costs "from the cradle to the grave"). From the manufacturer's perspective, TLCC integrates the following three life cycle concepts:

    A. The Research Development and Engineering (RD&E) Cycle has three stages:

        1. *Market research* to assess emerging customer needs, leading to idea generation for new products

        2. *Product design* (development of technical aspects of the product)

        3. *Product development* (incorporation of critical features and design of prototypes, production processes, and special tooling)

Exhibit 9-2 shows the relationship between **committed costs** (costs that a company knows it will have to incur at a future date) and costs incurred. A dollar spent

on activities in the RD&E stage can save $8 to $10 on manufacturing and post-manufacturing activities, such as design changes or service costs.

    B.   The Manufacturing Cycle: the cycle in which costs are incurred in the production of the product

        1.   During this stage, there is often little room for engineering flexibility to influence product costs and product design because they have been set in the previous cycle.

        2.   Operations management decisions, such as facilities layout or the implementation of JIT manufacturing, can help to reduce manufacturing life cycle costs.

        3.   Activity-based cost management can help identify opportunities to improve efficiency and reduce costs.

    C.   The Post-sale Service and Disposal Cycle: the cycle that begins once the first unit of product is in the hands of a customer. Thus, there is overlap with the manufacturing cycle. This cycle typically has three stages:

        1.   *Rapid growth* from the first shipment through the growth stage of the product's sales cycle.

        2.   *Transition* from the peak of the sales cycle to the peak in the service cycle.

        3.   *Maturity* from the peak in the service cycle to the time of the last shipment made to a customer. Disposal occurs at the end of a product's life and lasts until the final unit of the product is retired.

Exhibit 9-3 provides a breakdown of life cycle costs across four types of products.

Learning Objective 3: Explain target costing.

V.   Target Costing

    A.   **Target costing** is a method of profit planning and cost management used during the RD&E cycle to reduce manufacturing costs to targeted levels.

Exhibit 9-4 compares traditional cost reduction and Japanese target costing, and **Exhibit 9-5** provides a target-costing example.

B. **Traditional cost reduction** begins with market research into customer requirements, followed by product specification. At this stage, product cost is not a significant factor in product design. After the engineers and designers have determined product design, they estimate product cost (C_t), where the t subscript indicates numbers derived under traditional thinking. If the estimated cost is considered to be too high, then it may be necessary to modify product design. The desired profit margin (P_t) is computed by subtracting the estimated cost from the expected selling price (S_t). The profit margin in the traditional system is expressed with the following equation:

$$P_t = S_t - C_t$$

C. Under the **cost-plus method**, an expected profit margin (P_{cp}) is added to the expected product cost (C_{cp}), where the subscript cp indicates numbers derived from the cost-plus method. Selling price (S_{cp}) is the sum of these two variables. In equation form, this relationship for the cost-plus approach is expressed as:

$$S_{cp} = C_{cp} + P_{cp}$$

As in the traditional method described above, product designers do not attempt to achieve a particular cost target.

D. In **target costing**, both the sequence of steps and way of thinking about determining product costs differ significantly from traditional costing (see Column 2, Exhibit 9-4).

1. Unlike traditional costing approaches, market research in conjunction with target costing includes obtaining customer input continually throughout the target costing process.

2. Compared to traditional cost reduction, the target costing process devotes much more time at the product specification and design stage to minimize design changes during the manufacturing process.

3. The target costing process also focuses on minimizing the cost of ownership of a product over its useful life.

4. Determining a **target selling price** (S_{tc}) and **target product volume** depends on the company's perceived value of the product to the customer. The subscript tc indicates numbers derived in the target-costing approach.

5. The **target profit margin** (P_{tc}) results from a long-run profit analysis, often based on return on sales (net income/sales).

6. The **target cost** (C_{tc}) is the difference between the target selling price and the target profit margin:

$$C_{tc} = S_{tc} - P_{tc}$$

7. Once the target cost is set, the company must determine target costs for each component.

8. The **value engineering** process examines each component of a product to determine whether it is possible to reduce costs while maintaining functionality and performance. Several iterations of value engineering usually are needed before it is possible to determine the final target cost.

9. Throughout the process, cross-functional teams of individuals representing the entire value chain guide the process.

10. Suppliers play a critical role in successful target costing. **Supply chain management** is a management system that develops cooperative, mutually beneficial, long-term relationships between buyers and sellers.

E. Concerns about target costing include:

1. Conflicts can arise between parties (e.g., manufacturing and marketing) if the entire organization does not understand and commit to the target costing process.

2. Employees, especially design engineers, experience a great amount of pressure to meet goals, leading to burnout.

3. Development time may increase as a result of repeated value engineering cycles to reduce costs. This may slow time to market.

Learning Objective 5: Explain Kaizen costing.

VI. Kaizen costing

A. **Kaizen costing** is similar to target costing in its cost reduction mission, except that it focuses on the manufacturing stage of the total life cycle.

B. *Kaizen* means making improvements to a process through small, incremental amounts, rather than through large innovations.

C. There are fewer opportunities to effect major changes with Kaizen costing than with target costing because Kaizen costing occurs once the product and manufacturing process have been designed.

D. The **target reduction rate** is the ratio of the target reduction amount to the specified cost base. Kaizen costing's goal is to ensure that actual production costs are less than the cost base. However, the process includes assessing whether the cost of disruptions to production is greater than the savings due to Kaizen costing.

Exhibit 9-6 illustrates one approach to computing Kaizen costs for plants, and **Exhibit 9-7** compares standard costing to Kaizen costing.

    E.   **Kaizen costing** differs from traditional **standard costing** in the following ways:

        1.   Under standard costing, a cost control system concept is used, stability in current manufacturing processes is assumed, and the goal is to meet performance standards. However, under Kaizen costing, a cost reduction concept is used, continuous improvement in manufacturing is assumed, and the goal is to achieve cost reduction targets that are continually adjusted downward.

        2.   Under standard costing, standards are set annually or semiannually, cost variance analysis involves comparing actual to standard costs, and cost variance investigation occurs when standards are not met. Under target costing, cost reduction targets are set and applied monthly, and Kaizen methods are applied all year long to achieve targets.

        3.   In traditional standard costing, it is commonly assumed that managers and engineers have the best knowledge to reduce costs. Under Kaizen costing, workers who are closest to the process are thought to have the best insight into how cost should be reduced.

    F.   Concerns about Kaizen costing include:

        1.   Kaizen costing places enormous pressure on employees to reduce every possible cost. To address the problem, some Japanese automobile companies use a grace period, or *cost sustainment period*, in manufacturing just before a new model is introduced. This allows employees the chance to learn any new procedures before the company imposes Kaizen targets on them.

        2.   Kaizen costing may induce too much focus on details and too little attention to the overall system.

Learning Objective 6: Discuss environmental costing issues.

    VII.   Environmental Costing

        A.   **Environmental costing** is a costing system that computes the cost of the effects an organization has on the environment. Environmental costing involves selecting suppliers whose philosophy and practice in dealing with the environment matches the buyer's, as well as using other "green manufacturing" techniques.

    B.   Activity-based costing systems can provide information to help control and reduce environmental costs.

        1.   Identify activities that cause environmental costs.

        2.   Determine the costs associated with the activities

        3.   Assign the costs to products, distribution channels, and customers.

    C.   Environmental costs fall into two categories.

        1.   *Explicit costs* include the direct costs of modifying technology and processes, costs of cleanup and disposal, costs of permits to operate a facility, fines levied by government agencies, and litigation fees.

        2.   *Implicit costs* often relate to infrastructure required to monitor environmental issues. Examples include administration and legal counsel, employee education and awareness, and the loss of goodwill if environmental disasters occur.

Exhibit 9-8 portrays Bristol-Myers Squibb's approach to environmental health and safety in all phases of their products' life cycles.

Learning Objective 7: Understand the process of benchmarking the best practices of other organizations.

VIII.   Benchmarking

    A.   **Benchmarking** is the process of studying and comparing how other organizations perform similar activities and processes, then adapting the best practices of other organizations to improve the firm's own performance. The other organization can be internal or external to the firm and are selected because they are known to have excellent performance for the benchmarked process.

    B.   Benchmarking typically consists of the following five stages:

        1.   Internal study and preliminary competitive analyses

        2.   Developing long-term commitment to the benchmarking project and coalescing the benchmarking team

3. Identifying benchmarking partners. Critical factors include:

   a. *Size of the partners*, which will depend on the specific activity or method being benchmarked

   b. *Number of partners*

   c. *Relative position of the partners within and across industries*

   d. *Degree of trust among partners*, which is critical to obtaining truthful and timely information

4. Information gathering and sharing methods

   a. Type of information that benchmarking organizations collect

      i. Product benchmarking

      ii. Functional (process) benchmarking

      iii. Strategic benchmarking

   b. Methods of information collection

      i. **Unilateral (covert) benchmarking**: companies independently gather information about other companies that excel in the area of interest through industry trade associations or information clearing houses.

      ii. **Cooperative benchmarking**: information is shared voluntarily between parties.

         - **Database benchmarking**: companies pay a fee in order to gain access to information from a database operator

         - **Indirect/third-party benchmarking**: an outside consultant acts as a liaison among firms engaged in benchmarking

         - **Group benchmarking**: participants meet openly to discuss their methods

5. Taking action to meet or exceed the benchmark

Exhibit 9-9 provides many specific examples of factors that can be benchmarked in each of the five stages above.

PRACTICE TEST QUESTIONS AND PROBLEMS

True/False

_____ 1. The greatest opportunity to influence product costs and product design occurs in the manufacturing cycle.

_____ 2. The post-sale service and disposal cycle overlaps with the manufacturing cycle.

_____ 3. Total life cycle costing of a product includes costs incurred before, during, and after the manufacturing cycle.

_____ 4. Manufacturing organizations should focus their attention primarily on manufacturing costs, because manufacturing costs invariably constitute the largest percentage of total costs.

_____ 5. Benchmarking (or performance) gaps are determined only for quantitative measures related to manufacturing processes.

_____ 6. Kaizen costing and target costing both have a mission of cost reduction.

_____ 7. Kaizen costing is virtually identical to standard costing.

_____ 8. Industry leaders do not need to benchmark.

_____ 9. The terms *in control* and *out of control* apply only to manufacturing processes.

_____ 10. An organization developing benchmarking as it adopts a total life cycle costing approach should expect that a short-term commitment to benchmarking will be adequate.

Multiple-Choice

1. Which of the following is NOT part of the RD&E cycle?
   (a) Kaizen costing
   (b) Value engineering
   (c) Target costing
   (d) Market research

2. Traditional cost reduction involves all of the following, EXCEPT
   (a) market research into customer requirements.
   (b) estimation of product cost.
   (c) obtaining prices from suppliers.
   (d) value engineering.

3. Which of the following is NOT one of the four characteristics of relevant information?
   (a) Timely
   (b) Committed
   (c) Flexible
   (d) Consistent

4. Which of the following is NOT a critical factor in identifying benchmarking partners?
   (a) Industry of the partner
   (b) Size of the partners
   (c) Number of partners
   (d) Degree of trust among the partners

5. Which of the following is NOT true about benchmarking?
   (a) It requires that organizational members understand their current operations and approaches to conducting business.
   (b) It looks externally to practices of other organizations for guidance on improving.
   (c) It is often highly cost effective.
   (d) Only manufacturing processes can be benchmarked.

6. Which of the following is NOT an example of cooperative benchmarking?
   (a) Relying on aggregate or average data from industry trade associations
   (b) Purchasing information from a database operator who collects and edits the information prior to revealing it to users; the identity of the source of the data often is not revealed
   (c) Hiring an outside consultant to act as a liaison among firms engaged in benchmarking
   (d) Benchmarking by meeting with others to discuss methods

7. Which of the following is NOT a concern about target costing?
   (a) It can lead to conflicts among organization members.
   (b) Employees experience a great amount of pressure to meet goals, leading to burnout.
   (c) The marketing researchers in the organization will be unhappy because they have no role in the target costing process.
   (d) Time to market may be slowed because of repeated cycles of attempts to reduce costs.

8. Which of the following is NOT true about a standard costing system?
   (a) It is based on a cost control concept.
   (b) It assumes stability in the current manufacturing process.
   (c) The goal is to meet cost performance standards.
   (d) It assumes production workers have the best knowledge to reduce costs.

9. Which of the following is NOT true about target costing?
   (a) Suppliers play a critical role.
   (b) Market research includes obtaining customer input continually throughout the target costing process.
   (c) Little attention is devoted to minimizing design changes during the manufacturing process.
   (d) One focus is minimizing cost of ownership of a product over its useful life.

10. Which of the following would NOT be a result of the value engineering process?
    (a) A change in the product design
    (b) Replacement of some materials used in production
    (c) Redesign of manufacturing processes
    (d) Setting of a preliminary target cost for the product

Completion

1. _____ _____ _____ _____ provides information for managers to understand and manage costs through a product's design, development, manufacturing, marketing, distribution, maintenance, service, and disposal stages.

2. During the RD&E stage of the total life cycle of a product that requires discrete manufacturing processes and reasonably short product life cycles, _____ _____ is used as a method of cost planning that focuses on reducing costs.

3. _____ refers to the set of procedures, tools, performance measures, and systems that organization members use to guide and motivate all employees to achieve organizational objectives.

4. In the ____-____ method of pricing, an expected or desired profit margin is added to the expected product cost to arrive at the selling price.

5. The _____ _____ process examines each component of a product to determine whether it is possible to reduce costs while maintaining functionality and performance.

6. _____ means making improvements to a process through small, incremental amounts.

7. The five steps in the process of keeping an organization in control are: _____, _____, _____, _____, and _____.

8. In Kaizen costing, the _____ _____ _____, which is the ratio of the target reduction amount divided by the cost base, is applied to all variable costs.

9. The three broad classes of information on which firms benchmark are _____ benchmarking, _____ benchmarking, and _____ benchmarking.

10. Administration and legal counsel, employee education and awareness, and other costs related to infrastructure required to monitor environmental issues are examples of _____ environmental costs.

Problems

1. Why are control systems necessary for organizations?

2. Traditional cost-plus pricing has been labeled "cost up/price up," and target costing has been labeled "price down/cost down." Explain why these labels might be appropriate.

SOLUTIONS TO PRACTICE TEST QUESTIONS AND PROBLEMS

True/False

1. False. Product costs and product design are primarily set in the RD&E cycle.

2. True. The post-sale service and disposal cycle begins once the first unit of product is in the hands of a customer.

3. True. Total life cycle costing of a product includes costs incurred before, during, and after the manufacturing cycle.

4. False. Focusing only on manufacturing costs could cause organizations to ignore a significant proportion of RD&E or service and disposal costs.

5. False. Benchmarking gap analysis can include more qualitative measures and measures not directly associated with manufacturing processes.

6. True. Kaizen costing and target costing both have a mission of cost reduction. Kaizen costing occurs during the manufacturing stage, and target costing occurs during the RD&E stage.

7. False. Kaizen costing and standard costing are quite distinct (see Exhibit 9-7).

8. False. Industry leaders may benchmark because of their commitment to continuous improvement or in order to remain competitive. Moreover, industry leaders with respect to product lines can also benchmark processes not directly related to the product lines.

9. False. These terms describe whether a system is on a path leading to an organization's or unit's objectives, and therefore apply to manufacturing and nonmanufacturing settings.

10. False. Adopting a total life cycle costing approach involves significant organizational change that can take several years. Consequently, the commitment to benchmarking should be long term.

Multiple-Choice

1. a. Kaizen costing focuses on the manufacturing cycle.

2. d. Value engineering is associated with target costing.

3. b. The fourth characteristic of relevant information is "accurate."

4. a. The fourth critical factor in identifying benchmarking partners is relative position of the partners within and across industries. Benchmarking partners need not be in the same industry.

5. d. Nonmanufacturing processes can be benchmarked. For example, management accounting methods can be benchmarked.

6. a. Relying on aggregate or average data from industry trade associations is an example of unilateral benchmarking.

7. c. Market research is a vital component of the target costing process.

8. d. In traditional standard costing, it is assumed that managers and engineers have the best knowledge to reduce costs. The assumption that production workers have the best knowledge to reduce costs is characteristic of Kaizen costing.

9. c. The target costing process devotes considerable attention to minimizing design changes during the manufacturing process.

10. d. A preliminary target cost is set *before* the value engineering process begins.

Completion

1. Total life cycle costing

2. target costing

3. Control

4. cost-plus

5. value engineering

6. Kaizen

7. plan, execute (or implement), monitor, evaluate, correct

8. target reduction rate

9. product, functional (or process), strategic

10. implicit

Problems

1. Control systems serve a very important purpose in organizations. The planning function is quite meaningless without control. Control systems provide tools and methods that organizations use to assess and improve their progress towards achieving goals that are specified by the planning function. Generally, five steps are involved. First, goals are set and the processes to accomplish the goals are identified. Second, the plan is implemented. Third, the system's performance is measured, and fourth, differences between performance and goals are analyzed. Finally, any necessary corrective action is taken. The control system then cycles through the process again.

2. In traditional cost-plus pricing, estimated product costs plus an expected or desired profit margin yield the projected price. Therefore, if product cost is high, the projected selling price will also be high. That is, as "costs go up, prices go up."

   In target costing, a target selling price is determined, based on perceptions of the value of the product to the customer and on market conditions. The target profit margin is then subtracted from the target selling price to arrive at a target cost. Therefore, if perceptions are that prices must be relatively low, the product cost must also be relatively low in order to achieve the desired profit margin. That is, as "prices go down, costs must go down."

chapter 10

Motivating Behavior in Management Accounting and Control Systems

Learning Objectives

After reading this chapter, you will be able to

1. discuss the four key behavioral considerations in MACS design
2. explain the human resources model of management
3. discuss task and results control systems
4. apply the ethical control framework to decisions
5. understand the balanced scorecard and its applications
6. discuss the links between different incentive systems and performance

SUMMARY

This chapter discusses four key behavioral characteristics of a well-designed management accounting and control system (MACS). Briefly, the four characteristics pertain to including an ethical code, using an integrated set of performance measures, empowering employees, and developing appropriate incentive systems. The chapter describes the balanced scorecard as a performance measurement system that translates an organization's strategy into clear objectives, measures, and initiatives.

REVIEW OF KEY TERMS AND CONCEPTS

> Learning Objective 1: Discuss the four key behavioral considerations in MACS design.

I. Behavioral Characteristics of Well-Designed Management and Control Systems

    A. Embedding the organization's ethical code into MACS design

    B. Using a mix of short- and long-term qualitative and quantitative performance measures

    C. Empowering employees to be involved in decision making and MACS design

    D. Developing an appropriate incentive system to reward performance

Because human interests and **motivation** (an individual's interest or drive to act in a certain manner) can vary significantly, a major role for control systems is to motivate behavior congruent with the desires of the organization. Companies whose MACS displays the characteristics listed previously often believe in the human resource management model of motivation, described following.

> Learning Objective 2: Explain the human resources model of management.

II. Managerial Approaches to Motivation: Three Approaches

    A. **Scientific management school**: a management movement with the underlying philosophy that most people find work objectionable, that people care little for making decisions or showing creativity on the job, and that money is the driving force behind performance.

    B. **Human relations movement**: a managerial movement that recognizes that people have needs well beyond performing a simple repetitive task at work and that financial compensation is only one aspect of what workers desire.

    C. **The human resources model of motivation (HRMM)**: an approach to human motivation that introduces a high level of employee responsibility for and participation in decisions in the work environment. This managerial view emphasizes that individuals are creative, find work enjoyable, and desire to participate in developing objectives, making decisions, and attaining goals in their work environment. This chapter uses the human resources model as the basis for presentation of the four behavioral considerations in MACS design.

Learning Objective 1, continued:
Discuss the first of four key behavioral considerations in MACS design.

Learning Objective 4: Apply the ethical control framework to decisions.

III. The Organization's Ethical Code of Conduct and MACS Design

    A. **Ethics** is a discipline that focuses on the investigation of standards of conduct and moral judgment. To incorporate ethical principles into the design of a MACS design and help managers deal effectively with pressures to suspend ethical judgment, system designers might try to ensure the following:

        1. The organization has formulated, implemented, and communicated to all employees a comprehensive code of ethics. (Review *beliefs systems* in Chapter 1.)

        2. All employees understand the organization's code of ethics and the boundary systems that constrain behavior. (Review *boundary systems* in Chapter 1.)

        3. A system, in which employees have confidence, exists to detect and report violations of the organization's code of ethics.

    B. Most organizations attempt to address ethical considerations and avoid ethical dilemmas by developing a code of ethics. The **hierarchy of ethical principles** listed below, in descending order of authority, captures a broad array of ethical considerations.

        1. Legal rules

        2. Societal norms

        3. Professional codes (CPAs, and CMAs, for example)

        4. Organizational or group norms

        5. Personal norms

    C. Dealing with ethical conflicts

        1. One step in avoiding ambiguity or misunderstanding is to maintain a hierarchical ordering of authority; the organization's stated code of

ethics should not allow any behavior that is legally or socially unacceptable.

2. Another critical factor in reducing ethical conflicts is the way that the chief executive and other senior managers behave and conduct business.

3. The potential for ethical conflicts may arise with the code itself. The conflicts that appear most in practice are those between:

   a. The law and the organization's code of ethics

   b. The organization's practiced code of ethics and common societal expectations

   c. The individual's set of personal and professional ethics and the organization's practiced code of ethics

D. Different kinds of conflicts can arise for employees in an organization, including:

1. Conflicts between individual and organizational values.

2. Conflicts between the organization's stated and practiced values. Alternative four in the textbook, *delay taking action and work with respected leaders in the organization to change the discrepancy,* is one that is often recommended.

E. Elements of an effective **ethical control system** (a system that reinforces the ethical responsibilities of all firm employees)

1. A **statement** of the organization's values and code of ethics stated in practical terms, with examples

2. A clear statement of the employee's **ethical responsibilities** for every job description

3. Adequate **training** to help employees identify ethical dilemmas in practice and learn how to deal with those dilemmas

4. Evidence that senior management expects organization members to **adhere** to its code of ethics

5. Evidence that employees can make ethical decisions or report violations of the organization's stated ethics **without fear of reprisals** from superiors, subordinates, or peers in the organization

6. An ongoing **internal audit** of the efficacy of the organization's ethical control system

Review the seven steps in the Decision Model for Resolving Ethical Issues in **Exhibit 10-1**.

Learning Objective 3: Discuss task and results control systems.

IV. Motivation and Goal Congruence

    A. When designing jobs and specific tasks, system designers should consider the following three dimension of motivation:

        1. *Direction*, or the tasks on which an employee focuses attention

        2. *Intensity*, or the level of effort expended

        3. *Persistence*, or the duration of time an employee will stay with a task or job

    B. **Goal congruence** refers to the outcome when managers' and employees' goals are aligned with organizational goals.

    C. With complete goal congruence, employers might rely on **employee self-control**, a managerial method in which employees monitor and regulate their own behavior and perform to their highest levels. Regardless, management often relies on different forms of behavior control at work because different types of work tasks require different levels of skill, precision, and responsibility.

        1. **Task control** refers to the process of developing standard procedures that employees are told to follow.

            a. **Preventive control** focuses on preventing undesired events. Much if not all of the discretion is taken out of performing a task.

            b. **Monitoring** means inspecting the work or behavior of employees while they are performing a task.

        2. Results control methods focus on measuring employee performance against stated objectives. **Results control** is the process of hiring qualified people who understand the organization's objectives, telling them to do whatever they think best to help the organization achieve its objectives, and using the control system to evaluate the resulting performance, thereby assessing how well they have done.

Note the textbook's lists of situations in which task control and results control are most effective. **Exhibit 10-2** provides data on companies engaged in electronic monitoring.

Learning Objective 1, continued:
Discuss the second of four key behavioral considerations in MACS design.

Learning Objective 5: Understand the balanced scorecard and its applications.

V. Using a Mix of Performance Measures—The Balanced Scorecard Approach

    A. The need for multiple measures of performance

        1. **Gaming a performance indicator** refers to an activity in which an employee may engage in dysfunctional behavior to achieve a single goal.

        2. **Data falsification** is the process of knowingly altering company data in one's favor.

        3. To motivate desired behavior, organizations can design performance measurement systems with multiple performance measures that reflect the complexities of the work environment. Using multiple performance measures will help employees recognize the various dimensions of their work and to be less intent on trying to maximize their performance on a single target at the expense of other aspects of their jobs.

    B. Using a mix of quantitative performance measures

        1. **Quantitative financial measures** include cost, profit, and net income.

        2. **Quantitative nonfinancial measures** include yield, cycle time, schedule adherence, number of defectives, market share, and customer retention..

        3. **Qualitative measures** include image, reputation, and customer satisfaction. Some qualitative measures, such as customer satisfaction, can be quantified.

    C. The balanced scorecard

1. **The balanced scorecard** is a systematic performance measurement system that translates an organization's strategy into clear objectives, measures, targets, and initiatives organized by four perspectives:

    a. External **financial** measures for stakeholders and customers, such as return on capital employed, operating income, and economic value added

    b. **Customer** measures, such as retention, satisfaction, customer profitability, and market share

    c. **Internal business process** measures, such as cycle time

    d. **Learning and growth** measures, such as the number of new patents and the development of employee skills. This perspective addresses the three sources of organizational learning and growth: people, systems, and organizational procedures

2. The balanced scorecard integrates an organization's measures and helps organizations grapple with their intangible or intellectual assets. A company's intangible assets enable it to:

    a. Develop customer relationships, including retaining existing customers and reaching new customer segments

    b. Introduce innovative produces and services desired by targeted customer segments

    c. Produce high-quality, customized products and services at low cost and with short lead times

    d. Mobilize employee skills and motivation for continuous improvements in process capabilities, quality, and response times

    e. Deploy information technology, databases, and systems

Exhibit 10-3 diagrams the balanced scorecard as a framework to translate a strategy into operational terms. Note that objectives, measures, targets, and initiatives are specified for each of the four perspectives: financial, customer, internal business process, and learning and growth. **Exhibit 10-4** provides a sample scorecard for Cigna Property and Casualty.

> Learning Objective 1, continued:
> Discuss the third of four key behavioral considerations in MACS design.

VI. Empowering Employees to be Involved in MACS Design: Two Essential Elements

    A. Participation in decision making:

        1. Research suggests that employees who participate in decision making have higher morale and greater job satisfaction, which in turn may translate into increased productivity.

        2. Participation and communication between local and central offices, for example, results in transmission of critical information to which central management would otherwise not have access.

    B. Education to understand information

        1. Employees at all levels must understand the organization's performance measures and the way they are computed in order to be able to take actions that lead to superior performance.

        2. Organizations that foster an environment of continually mastering new skills are called learning organizations. For a MACS to function well, employees must be constantly reeducated as the system and its performance measures change.

> Learning Objective 1, continued: Discuss the fourth of four key behavioral considerations in MACS design.

> Learning Objective 6: Discuss the links between different incentive systems and performance.

VII. Developing Appropriate Incentive Systems to Reward Performance

    A. **Intrinsic rewards** are those that come from within an individual and reflect satisfaction from doing the job and the opportunities for growth that the job provides.

    B. **Extrinsic rewards** are explicit, usually financial, rewards that one person provides to another to recognize a job well done. The rewards include trips, cash bonuses, stock bonuses, and recognition in newsletters and on plaques.

C. There is much debate about what types and mix of rewards (intrinsic versus extrinsic rewards) should be used. On the one hand, some argue that not enough emphasis is placed on developing an environment from which intrinsic rewards for individuals can be derived. On the other hand, some claim that extrinsic rewards are the most motivating types of rewards and that people respond best to money and external recognition that is based on their performance. Each organization must decide on the type of work environment it would like to develop and the mix of both types of rewards.

D. Extrinsic rewards based on performance:

1. **Incentive compensation systems**, or pay-for-performance systems, are reward systems that provide monetary (extrinsic) rewards based on measured results. The systems are designed to motivate achieving, or exceeding, measured performance targets.

    a. Rewards can be based on *absolute performance*, as in piece-rate incentive schemes for the number of good products produced.

    b. Rewards also can be based on performance relative to a plan or to a comparable group. For example, a *relative performance* plan might pay a bonus to the top insurance salesperson each month.

E. Effective Performance Measurement and Reward Systems.
If the organization has decided to reward performance, six broad characteristics should be considered to ensure that the performance measurement system will be effective.

1. Individuals must understand their jobs and the reward system and believe that it measures what they control and contribute to the organization.

2. A careful choice must be made about whether the performance measurement system measures the employee's inputs, outputs, or a mix of the two.

3. The performance measurement system should reflect the organization's critical success factors and measure performance across a set of balanced and comprehensive measures, as proposed in the balanced scorecard.

4. The reward system must set clear standards for performance that employees accept.

5. The measurement system must be calibrated so that it can accurately assess performance.

6. Where appropriate, incentives should consider rewarding groups, rather than individuals.

F. Conditions favoring incentive compensation
Incentive compensation seems to work best in decentralized systems where employees are empowered and can use their skill and authority to react to situations and make decisions.

G. Incentive compensation and employee responsibility
Employees' compensation should reflect the nature of their responsibilities in the organization. For instance, those who work in daily operations should have rewards that are tied to short-term measures, such as customer service; those who work on long-term projects should be rewarded on measures such as long-term growth or process improvements.

H. Rewarding outcomes

1. Incentive compensation schemes tie rewards to the outputs of employee performance rather than to inputs such as effort.

2. Rewards can be based on inputs (such as time, knowledge, and skill level) in three situations:

    a. When it is impossible to measure outcomes consistently

    b. When outcomes are affected by factors beyond the employee's control

    c. When outcomes are expensive to measure

I. Managing incentive compensation plans
There is controversy over the management of compensation plans, especially at the senior executive level. The criticism is that senior executives have been overpaid for mediocre performance.

J. Types of incentive compensation plans
Compensation plans can be grouped into two broad classes. The first relies on internal measures (usually provided by the management accounting system), and the second relies on the organization's share price in the stock market.

1. A **cash bonus** (also called a lump-sum reward, pay for performance, and merit pay) is a payment method that pays cash based on some measured performance. Cash bonuses can be based on individual or group performance. The bonus can be fixed in amount and triggered when performance exceeds a target, or it can be proportional to the level of performance.

2. **Profit sharing** is a cash bonus system calculated as a percentage of an organization unit's reported profit and is a group incentive com-

pensation plan focused on short-term performance. A profit-sharing plan specifies the portion of the organization's reported profits available for sharing, the sharing formula, the employees who are eligible to participate in the plan, and the formula for each employee's share.

3. **Gainsharing** is a system for distributing cash bonuses from a pool when the total amount available for distribution as cash bonuses is a function of performance relative to some target. The gainsharing plan usually applies to a group of employees within an organization. The three most widely used gain sharing programs are:

   a. **Improshare** (Improved Productivity Sharing)
   The bonus pool is determined by calculating the difference between the target level of labor cost, given the level of production, and the actual labor cost.

   b. **Scanlon plan** (a form of gainsharing program)
   First a base ratio is calculated using past data.

   $$\text{Base ratio} = \frac{\text{Payroll costs}}{\text{Value of goods or services produced}}$$

   In any period in which the ratio of payroll costs to the value of production or service is less than the base ratio, the labor savings are added to the bonus pool. In the reverse situation, some organizations deduct the difference from the bonus pool. Periodically, the pool is apportioned between the company and the employees in the pool using specified proportions.

   c. **Rucker plan** (a form of gainsharing program)
   The Rucker plan also works on a ratio based on past data.

   $$\text{Rucker standard} = \frac{\text{Payroll costs}}{\text{Production value}}$$

   where production value = (net sales − inventory change − materials and supplies used).

   Similar to the Scanlon plan, when actual labor costs are less than the Rucker standard, the employees receive a bonus.

4. A **stock option** is a right to purchase a unit of the organization's stock at a specified price, called the option price. The general idea behind stock options is to motivate employees to act in the long-run interests of the organization by taking actions and making decisions that will increase the organization's market value.

Note the textbook's fuller discussion of the various incentive systems just outlined.

PRACTICE TEST QUESTIONS AND PROBLEMS

True/False

_____ 1. The scientific management school of motivation assumes that individuals have a great deal of knowledge and information to contribute to the organization, and that they are highly creative and responsible.

_____ 2. Three key dimensions of motivation are direction, intensity, and pertinence.

_____ 3. *Task control* is a process designed to motivate compliance with stated organization goals or unit objectives.

_____ 4. One element of an ethical control system is a clear statement of the employees' ethical responsibilities for every job description.

_____ 5. Ethical dilemmas at work can be resolved only in a court of law.

_____ 6. Developing and using both quantitative and qualitative information is a key characteristic of a well-designed MACS.

_____ 7. Gaming a performance indicator is an example of goal-congruent behavior.

_____ 8. If an employee observes management engaged in unethical behavior, the best course of action for the employee is to resign and make the issue public.

_____ 9. Receiving a plaque for one's performance is an extrinsic reward.

_____ 10. An example of a reward based on absolute performance is paying a salesperson a bonus for exceeding the average performance of the sales group.

_____ 11. Incentive compensation systems work best in organizations in which employees have the skill and authority to make decisions.

_____ 12. The rewards of employees who manage daily operations should be tied to short-term performance measures.

_____ 13. Most experts believe that organizations using incentive compensation should restrict the participation in the plans to only senior executives.

_____ 14. Studies have shown that monetary compensation is the only factor that affects employees' motivation.

_____ 15. A cash bonus is also called merit pay.

_____ 16. A stock option is the right to purchase a unit of the organization's stock at a specified price, called the option price.

Multiple-Choice

1. In which of the following situations would task control be least useful?
   (a) Operating nuclear-generating facilities
   (b) Handling large amounts of cash
   (c) Preparing food in a fast-food restaurant
   (d) A rapidly changing environment

2. Which of the following is NOT a characteristic of a well-designed MACS?
   (a) The system is designed from the point of view of top management.
   (b) Employees can participate and are empowered.
   (c) An ethical code of conduct is incorporated.
   (d) Reward systems are tied to performance.

3. The following are all characteristics of the human resources model of motivation, EXCEPT
   (a) people do not find work objectionable.
   (b) people want to participate in developing objectives.
   (c) people's primary motivation at work is to make as much money as possible.
   (d) people have a great deal of knowledge to contribute to the organization.

4. The elements of an effective ethical control system include all of the following, EXCEPT
   (a) a statement of the organization's values and code of ethics.
   (b) a sworn affidavit by each employee that he or she will not violate the code.
   (c) a clear statement of the employee's ethical responsibilities.
   (d) a statement by management that outlines the consequences for violating the code.

5. An example of a qualitative performance measure is
   (a) on-time delivery.
   (b) speed to market.
   (c) output per hour.
   (d) warmth of the hospital staff.

6. To provide a balanced scorecard, a performance measurement system should do all of the following, EXCEPT
   (a) monitor the causes of performance on the primary objectives.
   (b) provide information for external financial reporting.
   (c) monitor the causes of performance on the primary objectives.
   (d) provide understanding of how processes create results.

7. Which of the following is NOT an intrinsic reward?
   (a) Job satisfaction
   (b) Opportunity for personal development
   (c) Being named employee of the month
   (d) Pride of accomplishment

8. Which of the following is NOT needed in the effective design of a performance measurement and reward system?
   (a) Always design the reward system based on the performance of the individual.
   (b) Make sure all employees know their jobs.
   (c) Make sure employees understand the relationship between performance improvements and their effects on rewards.
   (d) Design the system to monitor and reward the organization's critical success factors.

9. Which of the following is NOT a reason that designing compensations contracts is difficult?
   (a) Outcomes often reflect the joint effect of a decision and environmental uncertainty.
   (b) Outcomes are often the result of the activities of many people.
   (c) There is considerable disagreement among experts about the precise effect of compensation on motivation.
   (d) A compensation contract for an individual can be based only on outcomes that the individual controls.

10. In the Scanlon plan, the base ratio is
    (a) payroll costs/Value of production or service.
    (b) payroll costs/Inventory turnover.
    (c) net cash inflow/Value of production or service.
    (d) net cash inflow/Net sales.

11. Under the Scanlon plan, Ideal Company's base ratio is 0.25. If payroll costs are $5,000,000 and the value of production is $18,000,000, how much money is added to the bonus pool?
    (a) $ 500,000.
    (b) $3,250,000.
    (c) $ 0.
    (d) $4,500,000.

12. Stock options are usually available for
    (a) all employees of a firm.
    (b) middle managers and higher-level executives.
    (c) operations manager and higher-level managers.
    (d) senior executives.

Completion

1. The three managerial approaches regarding motivation are _____ _____, _____ _____ _____, and _____ _____ _____ _____.

2. The hierarchy of ethical principles discussed in the textbook includes _____, _____, _____, _____, and _____ rules, norms, or codes of conduct.

3. One element of an effective ethical control system is providing for an ongoing _____ _____ of the efficacy of the organization's system.

4. _____ _____ refers to the process of developing standard procedures that employees are told to follow.

5. The balanced scorecard is a systematic performance measurement system that translates an organization's strategy into clear objectives, measures, targets, and initiatives organized by the following four perspectives: _____, _____, _____ _____ _____, and _____ _____ _____.

6. _____ rewards relate to the nature of the organization and the design of the job that people experience, and they come from inside the individual.

7. Incentive compensation systems, or _____-_____-_____ systems, are reward systems that provide monetary rewards based on measured results.

8. _____ _____ is a group incentive system for distributing cash bonuses, where the total amount available for distribution as cash bonuses is based on reported profit.

9. _____ is a group incentive system for distributing cash bonuses, where the total amount available is a function of performance relative to some target.

10. Improshare stands for _____ _____ _____.

11. The Rucker standard is the ratio of _____ _____ to _____ _____.

Problems

1. As a manager at the Ducksbury Company you have learned that one of your other managers has been falsifying production reports to include more inventory than has been produced. Given that you have decided to act on the matter, what steps should you follow in dealing with this situation?

2. You are charged with designing an incentive compensation scheme for a major airline. Fill in the following table listing the most appropriate incentive and the kind(s) of behavior that should be rewarded.

Type of Employee	Type of Incentive	Behavior to Reward
Senior Executive		
Pilot		
Flight Attendant		
Complaint Office Manager		
Maintenance Worker		

3. Contrast and compare the differences in cash bonuses, profit-sharing schemes, gain-sharing systems, and stock options.

SOLUTIONS TO PRACTICE TEST QUESTIONS AND PROBLEMS

True/False

1. False. The human resources model of motivation assumes that individuals have a great deal of knowledge and information to contribute to the organization and that they are highly creative and responsible. The scientific management school of motivation assumes that people find work objectionable and that they have little creativity to offer on the job.

2. False. The three elements are direction, intensity, and persistence. *Direction* refers to the tasks on which an employee focuses attention. *Intensity* refers to the level of effort expended. *Persistence* refers to the duration of time an employee will stay with a task or job.

3. False. *Task control* refers to the process of developing standard procedures that employees are told to follow. Task control includes *preventive control*, which focuses on preventing undesired events by taking most of the discretion out of performing a task, and *monitoring*, which means inspecting the work or behavior of employees while they are performing a task. *Results control* methods focus on motivating compliance with stated organization goals or unit objectives.

4. True. A statement of ethical responsibilities is essential.

5. False. Ethical dilemmas can be resolved within an organization as well as in court.

6. True. Both types of information are essential in a well-designed MACS.

7. False. Gaming a performance indicator, which refers to an activity in which an employee engages in dysfunctional behavior simply to obtain good results on the performance indicator, is an example of nongoal-congruent behavior when such behavior is not aligned with the overall objectives of the organization.

8. False. The textbook provides many other possible courses of action; resigning and making the issue public is usually not the best course of initial action.

9. True. A plaque is an example of an extrinsic reward, which is an explicit reward that one person provides to another to recognize a job well done.

10. False. Paying a salesperson a bonus for exceeding the average performance of the sales group is an example of a reward based on *relative performance*.

11. True. Incentive compensation systems work best in organizations in which employees have the skill and authority to make decisions.

12. True. For managing daily activities, using short-term rewards is the most appropriate.

13. False. Many experts agree that all employees should participate in one plan or another within the same organization.

14. False. Nonmonetary factors, such as the organization's general management style and various forms of special recognition, also motivate people.

15. True. Another name for a cash bonus is merit pay.

16. True. A stock option is the right to purchase a unit of the organization's stock at a specified price, called the option price.

Multiple-Choice

1. d. Task control, which is the process of developing standard procedures that employees are told to follow, is difficult to achieve in an environment that is rapidly changing.

2. a. The system should incorporate multiple views, not just top management's.

3. c. Although money is one motivator, it is not the primary motivator for many people in the human resources view. To many employees, other factors, such as internal satisfaction and expressing creativity are important motivators.

4. b. A sworn affidavit is not part of an ethical control system.

5. d. Warmth of the hospital staff is a qualitative measure. One cannot observe or measure warmth of staff directly, as one could with the amount of output per hour.

6. b. Although the balanced scorecard monitors external financial measures, the balanced scorecard is designed for internal management use rather than for external reporting.

7. c. Being named employee of the month is an extrinsic reward.

8. a. Reward systems should be based on the performance of individuals or groups, depending on the situation.

9. d. Compensation can also be based on inputs, group measures, or relative performance.

10. a. In the Scanlon plan, the base ratio is: Payroll costs/Value of production or service.

11. c. Under the Scanlon plan, money is added to the bonus pool only if the ratio of labor costs to production value is less than the base ratio. In this case, the ratio in the current period is $5,000,000/$18,000,000 or 0.28, which is higher than the base ratio of 0.25. Thus, no money is added to the bonus pool for the Ideal Company.

    Equivalently, one can compute the potential amount to be added to the bonus pool as: (value of production this period × base ratio) − actual payroll costs = ($18,000,000 × 0.25) − $5,000,000 = $4,500,000 = $5,000,000 < 0. Therefore, no money will be added to the bonus pool.

12. d. Stock options are usually available for senior executives only.

Completion

1. scientific management movement, human relations movement, human resources model of motivation

2. legal, societal, professional, organizational (and/or group), personal

3. internal audit

4. Task control

5. financial, customer, internal business process, learning and growth

6. Intrinsic

7. pay-for-performance

8. Profit sharing

9. Gainsharing

10. Improved Productivity Sharing

11. payroll costs, production value

Problems

1. There are several options. The first is to do nothing and ignore the situation. However, sooner or later your colleague will get caught. If you do nothing, you are also violating the code of ethics, as every employee has a responsibility to report violations of the code.

   Given that you want to do something, it is probably best to start by talking to employees in your organization whose job it is to deal with ethical issues. If no such employees exist or are available, you might start by using a decision model similar to the one described in Exhibit 10-1.

2. There are many ways to design an incentive scheme. The table illustrates some options. Bonuses listed in the table are based on how well each employee does on the behaviors that should be rewarded in the third column.

Type of Employee	Type of Incentive	Behavior to Reward
Senior Executive	Stock options; bonus	Leadership ability
Pilot	Market wage plus bonus	On-time arrival and safe flights
Flight Attendant	Market wage plus bonus	Customer satisfaction
Complaint Office Manager	Market wage plus bonus	Customer satisfaction
Maintenance Worker	Market wage plus bonus	Number of error-free flights

3. Cash bonuses are payments of cash based on performance related to a standard or target. Commonly, when a target is met, the bonus is awarded. Cash bonuses are one-time awards that are not part of an employee's base pay. Profit sharing is a cash bonus that reflects the performance of a unit within an organization or the performance

of the entire organization. Thus, profit sharing is focused on a group's short-term performance on a specific indicator. Gainsharing is a system that awards cash bonuses based on a group or team achieving beyond a set standard or target. The target is usually based on a base-period performance indicator. Examples of gainsharing include Improshare, Scanlon plans, and Rucker plans. Finally, stock options are usually used to motivate and focus senior executives in organizations. Stock options are intended to motivate senior executives to consider the long-term performance of their organization. The theory is that as the value of the organization increases, so will the market price of the stock. In turn, the market price of the stock will exceed the option price of the stock.

chapter 11

Using Budgets to Achieve Organizational Objectives

Learning Objectives

After reading this chapter, you will be able to

1. identify the primary role of budgets and budgeting in organizations

2. demonstrate the importance of each element of the budgeting process

3. explain the different types of operating budgets and financial budgets and their interrelationships

4. describe the way that organizations effectively use and interpret budgets

5. use cost-volume-profit analysis to evaluate the operating and financial consequences of alternative decisions

6. undertake what-if and sensitivity analyses—two important budgeting tools used by budget planners

7. identify the role of budgets in service and not-for-profit organizations

8. recognize the behavioral effects of budgeting on an organization's employees

SUMMARY

This chapter discusses various approaches to budgeting and describes how budgets support planning and control. The chapter begins by explaining the various components of a master budget, which is a set of operating and financial plans for the budget period. Additional topics include cost-volume-profit analysis (study of the relationships between cost behavior, volume, and profits) and sensitivity and what-if analysis. The chapter concludes by discussing important behavioral considerations in the budgeting process.

REVIEW OF KEY TERMS AND CONCEPTS

> Learning Objective 1: Identify the primary role of budgets and budgeting in organizations.

I. The Role of Budgets and Budgeting

   A. The **budgeting process** determines the planned level of most flexible costs (those that vary with activity levels in the organization).

   B. A **budget** is a quantitative expression of the money inflows and outflows that predicts the consequences of current operating decisions and reveals whether a financial plan will meet organizational objectives.

   C. **Budgeting** is the process of preparing budgets.

   D. Budgeting supports the management functions of planning and coordinating activities and communicates the organization's short-term goals to its members.

   E. The differences between actual results and the budget plan are called **variances**. Variances are part of a larger control system for monitoring results.

   F. Budgeting generally involves forecasting the demand for three types of resources over different time periods:

   1. Flexible resources that create variable or flexible costs. These can be acquired or disposed of in the short term

   2. Intermediate-term capacity resources that create capacity-related costs

   3. Long-term capacity resources that create capacity-related costs

 Exhibit 11-1 illustrates the key role that budgeting plays in planning and control.

> Learning Objective 2: Demonstrate the importance of each element of the budgeting process.

Learning Objective 3: Explain the different types of operating budgets and financial budgets and their interrelationships.

II. The Budgeting Process

   A. The **master budget** consists of operating budgets and financial budgets, usually for one year.

Exhibit 11-2 shows linkages among the many components of the budgeting process. The outline following refers to the boxes in this exhibit.

   B. An **operating budget** forecasts revenues and expenses during the next operating period and includes monthly forecasts of sales, production, and operating expenses. Firms may adapt the set of operating plans below, depending on their needs. (Box numbers below refer to Exhibit 11-2.)

   1. A **sales plan** (box 2) summarizes planned sales for each product.

   2. A **capital spending plan** (box 3) specifies the long-term capital investments, such as buildings and equipment, that must be made to meet activity objectives.

   3. A **production plan** (box 5) schedules all required production.

   4. A **materials purchasing plan** (box 7) schedules purchasing activities.

   5. A **labor hiring and training plan** (box 8) specifies the hiring, releasing, and training of people that the organization must have to achieve its activity objectives.

   6. An **administrative and discretionary spending plan** (box 9) includes administration, staffing, advertising, and research and development.

Exhibit 11-3 illustrates how one company combines operating and financial data that will be used to determine future operating budgets.

   C. A **financial budget** identifies the expected financial consequences of the activities summarized in the operating budgets. Financial budgets include:

   1. A statement of expected cash flows to:

      a. Plan when excess cash will be generated so that short-term investments can be made

Using Budgets to Achieve Organizational Objectives **165**

    b. Plan how to meet any cash shortages

  2. A projected balance sheet and a projected income statement to evaluate the financial consequences of decisions; these two projected statements are generally called **pro forma financial statements**.

Exhibit 11-4 diagrams processes in a glass plant that produces high volumes of high-quality, low-cost glass bottles. An understanding of operations is important in estimating the operating and financial consequences of operating plans.

> Learning Objective 4: Describe the way that organizations effectively use and interpret budgets.

 III. The Budgeting Process Illustrated: Ontario Tole Art, Buoy Division

Carefully go through the Ontario Tole Art, Buoy Division example to understand how the budgeting process works. Work through all of the exhibits, beginning with **Exhibits 11-5** and **11-6**.

  A. A **demand forecast** is an estimate of the sales demand at a specified selling price. The budgeting process is influenced strongly by the demand forecast.

  B. Planners match the completed sales plan with inventory policy and capacity level to determine a **production plan**.

  C. **Aggregate planning** is the process that compares the production plan with the amount of available productive capacity; this comparison assesses the feasibility of the proposed production plan.

  D. **Spending plans** are developed, for example, to purchase raw materials, hire and train new employees, and spend on administrative and discretionary items such as research and development and advertising. A **discretionary expenditure** is an expenditure whose short-term cost is not dictated directly by the proposed level of activities (e.g., advertising and research and development).

  E. There are three major types of resources that organizations acquire that will determine their level of monthly production capacity (see Exhibit 11-7):

    1. Flexible resources that the organization can acquire in the short term. Examples include materials.

    2. Capacity resources that the organization must acquire for the intermediate term. Labor is an example.

3. Capacity resources that the organization must acquire for the long term. Examples include plant and equipment.

F. Understanding the production plan involves the idea that production is the minimum of demand and capacity. In equation form, this is:

Production = Minimum (total demand, production capacity)

G. Financial plans include the projected balance sheet, income statement, and cash flow statement, which is organized into the following three sections:

1. Cash inflows

2. Cash outflows (Net cash flow = Cash inflows − Cash outflows)

3. Financing (Cash flows this period + Opening balance ± Changes = Closing balance). A **line of credit** with a financial institution is a short-term financing arrangement that allows an organization to borrow up to a specified limit at any time. A line of credit is *secured* if the organization has pledged an asset that the financial institution can seize if the borrower defaults on the line of credit provisions.

Continuing with the Ontario Tole Art, Buoy Division example, carefully review **Exhibits 11-9** to **11-14**, which include key financial statements.

H. Planners use budget information for the following:

1. *Identify broad resource requirements* to help develop plans to put needed resources in place

2. *Identify potential problems*, such as cash shortages

3. *Compare projected operating and financial results* with those of competitors as a general test of the efficiency of the organization's operating processes. Projected operating and financial results can also be compared with the organization's actual results, as discussed in Chapter 12.

Learning Objective 5: Use cost-volume-profit analysis to evaluate the operating and financial consequences of alternative decisions.

IV. Cost-Volume-Profit Analysis

A. Cost-volume-profit analysis is the process of combining cost behavior information with revenue information to project revenues, costs, and profits for different levels of volume.

B. Conventional cost-volume-profit analysis assumptions:

1. All organizational costs are either purely flexible or capacity related.

2. Units produced equal units sold.

3. Revenue per unit does not change as volume changes.

C. **Contribution margin per unit** is the difference between the revenue per unit and flexible (variable) cost per unit.

D. With the conventional assumptions listed, an organization's profit equation can be written as:

Profit = Revenue − Costs
Profit = (Units sold × Contribution margin per unit) − Capacity-related costs

E. **Break-even** sales volume is the sales volume where total sales revenue equals total cost. That is, profit = 0.

0 = (Units sold to break even × Contribution margin per unit) − Capacity-related costs,

or

Units sold to break even = Capacity-related costs ÷ Contribution margin per unit

F. A **cost-volume-profit chart** provides a visual way to display the relationships between volumes, revenues, costs, and profits.

Exhibit 11-16 displays a cost-volume-profit chart for the Ontario Tole Art example summarized in **Exhibit 11-15**.

G. Extending cost-volume-profit analysis for multiproduct organizations involves simulations on an electronic spreadsheet or using a weighted average contribution margin approach.

Exhibits 11-17, **11-18**, and **11-19** provide an example of multiproduct cost-volume-profit analysis.

Learning Objective 6: Undertake what-if and sensitivity analyses—two important budgeting tools used by budget planners.

---

168 Using Budgets to Achieve Organizational Objectives

V. What-If Analysis

   A. **What-if analysis** explores the effect of a change in one or more parameters on an outcome. Through this method, a number of questions can be raised concerning specific changes to variables and their effects on the key financial indicators.

Exhibit 11-20 presents a pro forma income statement showing the projected net income if a new machine is rented.

   B. **Sensitivity analysis** is the process of selectively varying a plan's or budget's key estimates to determine the effect on a decision rather than on an outcome. Sensitivity analysis allows planners to identify the estimates that are most critical for the decisions based on that model. If small changes in plan or model parameters (estimates and relationships) produce large changes in decisions, the plan or model is said to be *sensitive* to the estimates.

> Learning Objective 7: Identify the role of budgets in service and not-for-profit organizations.

VI. The Role of Budgeting in Service and Not-for-Profit (NFP) Organizations

   A. As in manufacturing organizations, budgeting helps nonmanufacturing organizations perform their planning function by coordinating and formalizing responsibilities and relationships and communicating the expected plans.

   B. In the natural resources sector, the key focus is on balancing demand with the availability of natural resources such as minerals or fish.

   C. In the service sector, the key focus is on balancing demand and the organization's ability to provide services, which is determined by the level and mix of skills in the organization. A key issue in planning in the service sector is the time needed to put skilled new people in place as needed.

   D. In NFP organizations, the traditional focus of budgeting has been to balance revenues. An **appropriation** is an authorized spending limit in a government department. Now, however, many governments are looking for ways to eliminate unnecessary expenditures and to make necessary expenditures more efficient, rather than just ensuring that government agencies do not spend more than authorized.

Exhibit 11-21 summarizes variations in the focus of budgeting in different types of organizations.

> Learning Objective 4, continued: Describe the way that organizations effectively use and interpret budgets.

VII. Periodic and Continuous Budgeting

A. A **periodic budget** is one that is prepared for a specified period of time, usually one year. As each budget period ends, the organization prepares a new budget for the next period.

B. **Continuous budgeting** is a process that plans for a specified period of time, usually one year, and organizes a budget into budget subintervals, usually a month or a quarter. As each budget subinterval ends, the organization drops the completed subinterval from the budget and adds the next budget subinterval.

VIII. Controlling Discretionary Expenditures

A. **Incremental budgeting** bases a period's expenditure level for a discretionary item on the amount spent for that item during the previous period. Incremental budgeting does **not**:

1. Require justification of the organization's goals for discretionary expenditures.

2. Include a provision to reduce or eliminate expenditures as the organization changes.

3. Have a mechanism to provide disproportionate support to discretionary items that will yield substantial benefits.

B. **Zero-based budgeting (ZBB)** requires that proponents of *discretionary* expenditures continually justify every expenditure. For each planning period, the starting point for each discretionary expenditure item is zero. This approach has been used primarily to assess government expenditures and, in profit-seeking organizations, has been applied only to discretionary expenditures such as research and development, advertising, and employee training.

C. **Activity-based budgeting** is based on the insights of activity-based costing. Activity-based budgeting uses knowledge about the relationship between production units and the activities required to produce those units. Major benefits of activity-based budgeting include:

1. It identifies situations when production plans require new capacity.

2. It provides a more accurate way to project future costs.

Exhibit 11-22 provides information for an activity-based budgeting example, illustrated in **Exhibit 11-23**.

    D. **Project funding** is a proposal for discretionary expenditures with a specific time horizon or sunset provision. Projects with indefinite lives are sometimes labeled *programs* and should be continuously reviewed to ensure that they are fulfilling their intended purposes.

Learning Objective 8: Recognize the behavioral effects of budgeting on an organization's employees.

IX. Behavioral Aspects of Budgeting: Two Interrelated Issues

    A. *Designing* the budget process: How should budgets be determined, who should be involved in the process, and at what level of difficulty should the budget be set to have the greatest positive influence on people's motivation and performance?

        1. **Authoritative budgeting** occurs when superiors simply tell subordinates what their budgets will be.

            a. Advantages include efficiency and coordination.

            b. Disadvantages include superiors' lack of knowledge of appropriate budget targets, possible lack of employee motivation and commitment to the budgeted goals because of no employee participation in establishing the budget, and motivational problems arise when resource commitments are insufficient to achieve high goals that have been set.

            c. Research shows that the most motivating types of budgets are those that are tight, that is, targets that are perceived as ambitious but attainable. **Stretch targets** exceed the previous targets by a significant amount and usually require an enormous increase in performance during the next budgeting periods. **Stretch budgeting** means that the organization will attempt to reach much higher goals with the current budget. Some believe that major innovations will result.

        2. **Participative budgeting** involves a joint decision-making process in which all parties agree about setting budget targets. Advantages include greater employee commitment to the budget, higher motivation to attain goals and keep within the budget, and employee communication of *private information* or *data* that can be incorporated in the budgeting process.

3. **Consultative budgeting** occurs when managers ask subordinates to discuss their ideas, but no joint decision making occurs. Managers later determine the budget. This is a practical method for large organizations, but **pseudoparticipation** can arise if management is not sincere in its desire to incorporate subordinates' input. Pseudoparticipation can have a debilitating effect on subordinates.

B. *Influencing* the budget process: How do people try to influence or manipulate the budget to their own ends?

1. Managers play **budgeting games** in which they attempt to manipulate information and targets to achieve as high a bonus as possible.

2. One consequence of the participation process in budgeting is that subordinates may ask for excess resources above what they need to accomplish their budget objectives. They may also understate their performance capabilities when given the opportunity so that they will be able to work under an easier budget. Both of these acts are referred to as creating **budget slack**.

The "Oh the (Budgeting) Games People Play Now, Every Night and Every Day Now, Never Meaning What They Say, Never Saying What They Mean" In-Practice box in this section of the textbook provides a humorous look at budgeting games.

PRACTICE TEST QUESTIONS AND PROBLEMS

True/False

_____ 1. The master budget consists of two general types of budgets: operating budgets and financial budgets.

_____ 2. The materials purchasing plan is part of the financial budget.

_____ 3. An administrative and discretionary spending plan includes administration, staffing, advertising, and research and development.

_____ 4. Asking for excess resources above what is needed to accomplish budget objectives and understating performance capabilities are both referred to as creating budget slack.

_____ 5. Stretch budgeting is unlikely to have any negative repercussions.

_____ 6. The contribution margin per unit is the difference between unit sales price and unit fixed cost.

_____ 7. Research shows that the most motivating types of budgets are those that are "tight" (ambitious but attainable).

_____ 8. What-if analysis explores the effect of a change in one or more parameters on an outcome.

_____ 9. A common format used in the financing section of the cash flow statement is: Cash flows this period + Opening balance ± Changes = Closing balance.

_____ 10. Zero-based budgeting and incremental budgeting are essentially the same method of budgeting.

Multiple-Choice

1. Budgeting requires the following kinds of skills, EXCEPT
   - (a) experience in forecasting.
   - (b) a knowledge of how activities affect costs.
   - (c) the ability to see how the organization's different activities fit together.
   - (d) experience in operations management.

2. Operating budgets or plans include the following, EXCEPT
   - (a) sales plan.
   - (b) capital spending plan.
   - (c) cash flow plan.
   - (d) labor hiring and training plan.

3. A demand forecast is
   - (a) an estimate of market demand given a product price.
   - (b) developed largely because of customer dissatisfaction.
   - (c) an estimate of market demand given the amount sold in the previous year.
   - (d) an estimate for the demand for labor.

4. A comparison of the production plan to productive capacity, taking into account the sales plan and inventory policy, is called
   - (a) discretionary planning.
   - (b) aggregate planning.
   - (c) demand planning.
   - (d) flexible planning.

5. Which of the following is not a type of resource used to determine monthly production capacity?
   - (a) Flexible resources acquired for the short term
   - (b) Capacity resources acquired for the intermediate term
   - (c) Fixed resources acquired for the short term
   - (d) Capacity resources acquired for the long term

6. Fireball Company has fixed costs of $318,000. It charges $25 for each product and each product's variable cost is $13. What is the break-even point in units?
   - (a) 12,720 units
   - (b) 26,500 units
   - (c) 8,369 units
   - (d) 24,462 units

Using Budgets to Achieve Organizational Objectives **173**

7. If forecasting errors have a critical effect on the production plan, planners say that the model is _____ to that estimate.
   (a) related
   (b) sensitive
   (c) unrelated
   (d) insensitive

8. Financial budgets include the following, EXCEPT a
   (a) projected balance sheet.
   (b) production plan.
   (c) cash flow plan.
   (d) projected income statement.

9. Which of the following is NOT true about activity-based budgeting?
   (a) It is applied only to discretionary expenditures, such as research and development.
   (b) It uses knowledge about the relationship between production units and the activities required to produce those units.
   (c) It identifies situations when production plans require new capacity.
   (d) It projects future costs more accurately than other budgeting methods.

10. Sunset provisions are associated with _____ _____.
    (a) incremental budgeting.
    (b) zero-based budgeting.
    (c) project funding.
    (d) continuous budgeting.

Completion

1. The three most common methods of setting budgets are known as _____, _____, and _____.

2. The _____ method of budget setting involves a joint decision-making process in which all parties agree about setting the budget targets.

3. The _____ spending plan specifies the long-term capital investments, such as buildings and equipment, that must be made to meet activity objectives.

4. A _____ budget is one that is prepared for a specified period of time, usually a year.

5. Paint and packing supplies are examples of _____ resources.

6. In the service sector, _____, rather than machines, usually represent the capacity constraint, underscoring the importance of budgeting even in nonmanufacturing organizations.

7. _____ – _____ financing is usually undertaken using a line of credit established with a financial institution.

8. At the break-even point, total _____ _____ equals total cost.

9. Government agencies call planned cash outflows, or authorized spending limits, _____.

10. The two major interrelated behavioral issues in budgeting are _____ the budget process and _____ the budget process.

Problems

1. Write an essay on the purpose and usefulness of budgeting.

2. Operating budgets have a number of specific types of plans associated with them. Describe each plan and its purpose.

3. The Chow Company manufactures and sells small toys to be put into cereal boxes. Price and cost data for Chow's operations are:

Costs per 100 Toys	
Selling price	$50
Variable Costs:	
Raw materials	$15
Direct labor	12
Manufacturing support	8
Selling expenses	2
Total variable costs per unit	$37
Annual fixed costs	
Manufacturing support	$160,000
Selling and administrative	120,000
Total fixed costs	$380,000
Estimated sales volume	500,000 toys

(a) What is Chow Company's break-even point?

(b) How many toys must Chow sell to make a target profit of $175,000?

SOLUTIONS TO PRACTICE TEST QUESTIONS AND PROBLEMS

True/False

1. True. The two general types of budgets are operating and financial budgets.

2. False. The materials purchasing plan is part of the operating budget.

3. True. An administrative and discretionary spending plan includes administration, staffing, advertising, and research and development.

4. True. Both these activities create budget slack.

5. False. Stretch budgeting means that the organization will try to reach much higher goals with the current budget. Although major innovations in processes, products, or services may result, workers may become frustrated or burned out, causing them to quit their jobs or simply stop trying to meet the targets.

6. False. The contribution margin is the difference between unit sales price and unit flexible (variable) cost.

7. True. Standards or budgets that are too "loose" (easy to achieve) provide little motivation, but standards that are impossible to achieve can cause people, out of frustration, to stop working hard.

8. True. *What-if analysis* explores the effect of a change in one or more parameters on an outcome. Compare this definition to that of *sensitivity analysis*, which is the process of selectively varying a plan's or budget's key estimates to determine the effect on a decision rather than on an outcome.

9. True. This format is a summary statement of the financing section of the cash flow statement.

10. False. Zero-based budgeting assumes the starting point for each discretionary expenditure item is zero, and incremental budgeting assumes the starting point is the amount spent on the item in the previous budget.

Multiple-Choice

1. d. Operations management skill is not required for budgeting.

2. c. A cash flow plan is included in the financial budget, not in the operating budget.

3. a. A demand forecast is an estimate of market demand given a product price.

4. b. Aggregate planning is the process that compares the production plan with the amount of available productive capacity; this comparison assesses the feasibility of the proposed production plan.

5. c. Fixed resources acquired for the short term are not a type of resource used to determine monthly production capacity.

6. b. The break-even point in units = Fixed costs divided by contribution margin per unit, or $318,000/($25 − 13) = 26,500$ units.

7. b. The key idea is that the model is sensitive to that estimate.

8. b. The production plan is part of the operating budget, not the financial budget.

9. a. *Incremental budgeting* is used only for discretionary items. Activity-based budgeting is used much more broadly.

10. c. Sunset provisions are associated with project funding, which is a proposal for discretionary expenditures with a specific time horizon or sunset provision.

Completion

1. authoritative, participative, consultative

2. participative

3. capital

4. periodic

5. flexible

6. people

7. Short-term

8. sales revenue

9. appropriations

10. designing, influencing

Problems

1. Your answer should include the following elements:

    (a) Budgets are summaries of expected outcomes of an organization's short-term operating activities and are a mechanism for communicating these goals to its members.

    (b) Budgets should reflect the key features and activities of the organization and are essentially a model of how these activities are tied together in the organization.

    (c) Budgets serve a number of purposes, including organizational planning and control. Control involves coordination, identifying and solving problems, and setting a standard of performance for motivation purposes.

2. There are a number of different plans that make up an operating budget. These include:

    (a) A *sales plan,* which identifies the planned level of sales for each product or service

(b) A *capital spending plan*, which details when long-term capital investments such as plant and equipment must be made to meet objectives

(c) A *production plan*, which identifies all required production

(d) A *materials purchase plan*, which schedules all required purchasing activities

(e) A *labor hiring and training plan*, which schedules the number, hiring, and training of people

(f) An *administrative and discretionary spending plan*, which includes staffing, research and development, and advertising plans

3. (a) Chow Company's break-even point can be calculated as follows:

$50 − 37 = $13 contribution per 100 toys
Contribution margin per toy = $0.13
Total fixed costs = $380,000
Break-even point is $380,000/0.13 = <u>2,923,077 toys</u>

(b) Let X = the number of toys that must be sold in order to earn $175,000

$X = (\$380,000 + \$175,000)/0.13 =$ <u>4,269,231 toys</u>

chapter 12

Responsibility Centers and Financial Control

Learning Objectives

After reading this chapter, you will be able to

1. describe the form and nature of variance analysis and apply its basic insights

2. explain why organizations use responsibility centers

3. identify the issues to consider and basic tools to use in assessing the performance of a responsibility center

4. describe the common forms of responsibility centers

5. assess the issues and problems created by revenue and cost interactions in evaluating the performance of an organization unit

6. identify the transfer-pricing alternatives available to organizations and the criteria for choosing a transfer-pricing alternative

7. use return on investment and economic value added as financial control tools

8. identify the limitations of financial controls

SUMMARY

This chapter discusses issues relating to financial control, which uses financial numbers as performance measures and involves comparing actual financial numbers with targets to derive variances. The first part of the chapter discusses cost variance analysis, or various comparisons of actual and budgeted costs. Next, the chapter describes performance assessment of responsibility centers such as cost centers, profit centers, and investment centers. Related issues include transfer pricing alternatives and measures of return on investment.

REVIEW OF KEY TERMS AND CONCEPTS

> Learning Objective 1: Describe the form and nature of variance analysis and apply its basic insights.

I. Variance Analysis

    A. **Variance analysis** is a set of procedures used by managers to help them understand the source of differences (variances) between actual and budgeted costs.

    Exhibits 12-1 through **12-9** illustrate the variance concepts and computations described following for a cellular phone service company.

    B. A master budget summarizes budgeted costs (also referred to as estimated, projected, target, or forecasted costs), which depend on three elements:

        1. The projected volume of activity, such as number of customers.

        2. The standards for the use of each of the budgeted items.

        3. The standards for the cost per unit of each of the budgeted items.

    C. A **first-level variance** for cost items is the difference between actual and master budget costs for that cost item. Exhibit 12-3 illustrates the computation for Canning Cellular's direct material, direct labor, and support costs.

        1. A **favorable variance**, denoted by an "F," means that actual costs were less than estimated costs.

        2. An **unfavorable variance**, denoted by a "U," means that actual costs were greater than estimated costs.

    D. **Second-level variances** are the planning variance and flexible budget variance, which sum to the first-level variance.

        1. A **flexible budget** is the forecast of the projected level of cost given the volume and mix of activities undertaken (see Exhibit 12-4)

        2. **Planning variances** are the cost differences between the master budget and the flexible budget, and reflect the difference between planned and actual output (see Exhibit 12-5).

3. **Flexible budget variances** show the difference between the flexible budget and the actual results. That is, the flexible budget variances reflect variances from the target level of costs *adjusted for the achieved level of activity* (see Exhibit 12-5).

E. **Third-level variances**: use and price variances

1. *Flexible budget variances* reflect both efficiency or **use variances** (the difference between the planned and actual use rates per unit of output) and cost or rate or **price variances** (the difference between the cost or price per unit of the various cost items).

2. The **material use variance** is:

$$(AQ - SQ) \times SP$$

where

AQ = actual quantity of materials used
SQ = estimated or standard quantity of materials required
SP = estimated or standard price of materials

3. The **material price variance is**:

$$(AP - SP) \times AQ$$

where

AP = actual price of materials
SP = estimated or standard price of materials
AQ = actual quantity of materials used

4. The sum of the material use and price variances is the **total material variance**, or actual cost minus flexible budget cost.

$$\text{Use variance} + \text{Price variance} = (AQ - SQ) \times SP + (AP - SP) \times AQ$$
$$= (AP \times AQ) - (SQ \times SP)$$

5. The direct labor **efficiency variance** is:

$$(AH - SH) \times SR$$

where

AH = actual number of direct labor hours
SH = estimated or standard number of direct labor hours
SR = estimated or standard wage rate

6. The direct labor **wage rate variance** is:

$$(AR - SR) \times AH$$

where

AR = actual wage rate
SR = estimated or standard wage rate
AH = actual number of direct labor hours

7. The sum of the direct labor efficiency and wage rate variances is the **total direct labor variance**, or actual cost minus flexible budget cost.

$$\text{Wage rate variance} + \text{Efficiency variance}$$
$$= (AH - SH) \times SR + (AR - SR) \times AH$$
$$= (AR \times AH) - (SR \times SH)$$

8. The flexible budget variance for flexible support costs can also be decomposed into use and price variances (see Exhibits 12-6 through Exhibit 12-9). In Exhibit 12-9, the first two lines of computation compute efficiency (use) and price variances using the blended costs per hour in Exhibits 12-8 and 12-9:

Use variance for system activation support = $(AH - SH) \times SR$
Price variance for system activation support = $(AR - SR) \times AH$

where (see Exhibits 12-4, 12-7, and 12-8)

AH = 0.12 hours per customer × 1,100,000 customers
SH = 0.15 hours per customer × 1,100,000 customers
AR = 325 per hour
SR = 300 per hour

Note that

Use variance + Price variance = 9,900,000F + 3,300,000U
$\qquad$ = 6,600,000F
$\qquad$ = Flexible budget variances for system activation in Exhibit 12-5

The last four lines of computation in Exhibit 12-9 provide a further decomposition of the system activation flexible budget variance and sum to 6,600,000F. The variances are computed as follows:

Due to additional labor (technical staff) use = $(AH - SH) \times SR$
Due to additional labor (technical staff) rate = $AH \times (AR - SR)$

where (see Exhibits 12-4, 12-7, and 12-8)

AH = 0.12 hours per customer × 1 × 1,100,000 customers
SH = 0.15 hours per customer × 1 × 1,100,000 customers
AR = 55 per hour
SR = 40 per hour

Due to additional computer use (computer hours per labor hour)
= $(AH - SH) \times SR$
Due to additional access rate (per computer hour) = $AH \times (AR - SR)$
where (see Exhibits 12-4, 12-7, and 12-8)

AH = 0.12 hours per customer × .45 × 1,100,000 customers
SH = 0.15 hours per customer × .5 × 1,100,000 customers
AR = 600 per hour
SR = 520 per hour

Learning Objective 2: Explain why organizations use responsibility centers.

II. Decentralization

A. **Centralized** organizations reserve most of the decision-making power for senior executives. Centralization is best suited to organizations that are well adapted to stable environments in which technology customer requirements are well understood, and the product line consists mostly of commodity products for which the most important attributes are price and quality.

B. **Decentralized** organizations delegate a great deal of decision-making authority to lower-level managers. Three conditions are necessary for effective decentralization:

1. Employees must be given, and must accept, the authority and responsibility to make decisions.

2. Employees must have the training and skills they need to accept the decision-making responsibility.

3. The organization must have a system in place that guides and coordinates the activities of decentralized decision makers.

Learning Objective 3: Identify the issues to consider and basic tools to use in assessing the performance of a responsibility center.

> Learning Objective 4: Describe the common forms of responsibility centers.

III. Basic Issues and Tools

    A. **Operations control** is the process of providing feedback to employers and their managers about the efficiency of activities being performed. That is, operations control views control from the point of view of process improvements and focuses on finding the best operating decisions.

    B. **Financial control** is a process used to assess an organization's financial success by measuring and evaluating its financial outcomes. Common financial measures include revenue, cost, profit, return on investment, and economic value added. Financial control signals when operations control is not working well and needs to be evaluated and improved.

    C. Effective control requires aligning the two perspectives of operations control and financial control.

IV. Responsibility Centers

    A. A **responsibility center** is an organization unit for which a manager is made responsible.

    B. A manager and supervisor establish responsibility center goals that should be specific and measurable, and should promote the long-term interests of the larger organization.

    C. Financial results are aggregate measures of performance; nonfinancial results can help managers identify the causes or drivers of the financial results.

    D. A **cost center** is a responsibility center in which employees control costs but do not control revenues or investment level.

        1. Comparing budgeted and actual results: Recall that a cost variance is the actual cost minus the budgeted cost. When actual costs are greater than budgeted costs, the variance is labeled unfavorable, but when the budgeted costs are greater than actual costs, the variance is labeled favorable.

Exhibit 12-10 provides a master budget, **Exhibit 12-11** provides actual results, and **Exhibit 12-12** illustrates an inappropriate comparison (variance analysis) between actual costs for one set of production levels, and budgeted costs for a different set of production levels. The flexible budget concept provides a more appropriate variance analysis.

2. The flexible budget: The key concept in flexible budgeting is that cost targets in the planned or master budget are recast to reflect the actual level of production. This allows comparisons of costs by holding volume constant. Flexible budget variances are the focus of cost control in a cost center.

3. Cost center performance measures should reflect not only costs, but also contributions the cost center makes to the organization's success. Possible additional performance measures include quality and response time.

Exhibit 12-13 presents a flexible budget for Moncton Carpet Products, and **Exhibit 12-14** reconciles the actual cost to the master budget target through the flexible budget.

E. A **revenue center** is a responsibility center in which members control revenues, but do not control manufacturing or acquisition costs of the products or services they sell or the level of investment made in the responsibility center.

1. When revenue centers have control over sales and marketing costs, those costs may be deducted from the revenue center's sales revenue to compute net revenue.

2. Revenue center employees can control the mix of items carried in their stores, prices of products, and promotional activities.

3. Revenue center managers are often at the mercy of others who determine the costs of their goods (e.g., service station managers have no control over the cost of the gas they sell).

4. Focusing only on revenues may cause managers to increase the use of activities that create costs in order to promote higher revenue levels.

F. A **profit center** is a responsibility center in which managers and other employees control revenues and costs of the products or services they deliver, but not the level of investment. The level of investment is usually controlled by senior management.

G. An **investment center** is a responsibility center in which the manager and other employees control revenues, costs, and the level of investment in the responsibility center. The investment center is like an independent business.

Exhibit 12-15 summarizes the differences among the various types of responsibility centers.

Responsibility Centers and Financial Control **187**

Learning Objective 5: Assess the issues and problems created by revenue and cost interactions in evaluating the performance of an organization unit.

V. Evaluating Responsibility Centers

A. The **controllability principle** states that the manager of a responsibility center should be assigned responsibility only for the revenues, costs, or investment that responsibility center personnel control. One major difficulty in applying this occurs when revenues and costs are jointly earned or incurred. Separating these component revenues and costs can involve intricate, and sometimes arbitrary, accounting procedures.

B. Some people argue that controllability is not the criterion that should be used in selecting a performance measure. Instead, the choice of performance measures should influence decision-making behavior. For example, performance measures might be chosen to motivate managers to find actions that can influence incurred costs or generated revenues.

C. An organization unit's **segment margin** measures its controllable contribution to the organization's profit and other indirect costs.

Exhibit 12-16 provides an example of a quarterly segment margin report for Earl's Motors. Note the format of the report and the breakdown of costs to arrive at the segment margins:

	Segment 1 ...	Segment 5	Total
Revenue	xxxx	xxxx	xxxx
- Variable costs	xxxx	xxxx	xxxx
Contribution margin	xxxx	xxxx	xxxx
- Other costs	xxxx	xxxx	xxxx
Segment margin	xxxx	xxxx	xxxx
- Allocated avoidable costs	xxxx	xxxx	xxxx
Income	xxxx	xxxx	xxxx
- Unallocated costs			xxxx
Dealership profit			xxxx

Allocated avoidable costs are the organization's administrative costs. These costs can be avoided if the unit is eliminated and the organization has time to adjust its capacity levels by selling excess facilities or by reducing the number of administrative staff.

The organization's *unallocated costs* (sometimes called *shutdown costs*), which are administrative and overhead costs incurred regardless of the scale of operations, are deducted from the total of the five segment (profit center) incomes to arrive at the dealership profit.

D. A unit's *segment margin* is an estimate of its short-term effect on the organization's profit and the immediate negative effect on the organization's profit if the unit is shut down.

E. A unit's *income* is an estimate of the long-term effect of the unit's shutdown on the organization's profit after fixed capacity is allowed to adjust.

F. Evaluation of segment margin numbers may involve comparison with:

1. Past performance

2. Comparable organizations

3. Absolute amounts (of costs and revenues, for example)

4. Relative amounts (such as percentage of revenue)

G. Segment margins should be interpreted carefully because:

1. Segment margins can represent highly aggregated summaries of each organizational unit's performance. Other critical success factors should be used as well to assess performance.

2. Some segment reports contain numbers that can be arbitrary because they rest on subjective revenue and cost allocation assumptions over which there can be legitimate disagreement. Accountants call these *soft numbers*.

Exhibit 12-17 provides an example of expensive processes involved in producing multiple products.

3. The revenue figures often reflect assumptions and allocations that can be misleading. These assumptions relate to the transfer-pricing issue—how the revenues that the organization earned are divided among the responsibility centers.

Learning Objective 6: Identify the transfer-pricing alternatives available to organizations and the criteria for choosing a transfer-pricing alternative.

VI. Transfer Pricing

A. **Transfer pricing** is the set of rules an organization uses to assign the prices to products transferred between internal responsibility centers.

1. Transfer pricing can be very arbitrary, especially if a high degree of interaction exists among the various responsibility centers.

 Exhibit 12-18 shows the possible interactions among the responsibility centers at Earl's Motors.

2. Transfer prices may serve different purposes, but the usual goal is to motivate the decision maker to act in the organization's best interests.

B. Four Major Approaches to Transfer Pricing

1. Market-based transfer prices

a. Market prices provide an independent valuation of products or services that are transferred between responsibility centers. If external markets exist for the intermediate product or service, then market prices are the most appropriate basis for pricing the transferred good or service.

b. Unfortunately, clear market prices often do not exist for many products or services.

2. Cost-based transfer prices

a. If goods or services do not have clear market prices, transfer prices are often based on cost.

b. Common cost-basis methods include variable cost, variable cost plus a markup, full cost, full cost plus a markup, and a dual rate. In the *dual-rate approach*, the receiving division is charged for the variable costs of producing the units supplied and the supplying division is credited with the net realizable value of the units supplied.

c. Cost-based transfer prices raise complex performance measurement, equity, and behavioral issues. Concerns about cost-based transfer prices include:

(1) Economists argue that only marginal-cost transfer prices are optimal and that any other method results in economic losses for the overall organization.

(2) Cost-based transfer does not focus on the intent of the transfer-pricing system, which is to allow computation of unit incomes.

(3) Cost-based transfer does not provide incentives to the supplying division to control costs, because the supplier can always recover its costs. One solution to this problem is to use standard cost as the transfer price.

(4) Organizations may find it difficult to compute a product's cost in a reasonably accurate way.

(5) Cost-based transfers do not provide the appropriate economic guidance when operations are capacity-constrained.

d. Cost allocations to support financial control: Even with all of the problems with evaluating responsibility center income statements, many organizations want to develop the statements. Each must be studied carefully and with healthy skepticism. Key issues involve allocating jointly incurred costs and revenues and understanding interrelationships among responsibility centers. Finding the most appropriate cost driver requires careful analysis.

See **Exhibits 12-19** and **12-20** on Shirley's Grill and Bar and the related discussion for examples of assignment of indirect costs to segments.

3. Negotiated transfer prices

a. When market prices do not exist, some organizations allow supplying and receiving responsibility centers to negotiate transfer prices. Critics argue that these types of prices reflect both negotiating skills and economic considerations, not just economics alone.

b. In an economic sense, the optimal transfer price occurs when the purchasing division offers to pay the supplying division the **net realizable value** of the last unit supplied for all of the units supplied. The net realizable value is the difference between a product's selling price and the additional costs needed to prepare the final product for sale.

4. Administered transfer prices

a. An arbitrator or a manager who applies some policy sets *administered transfer prices*.

b. Administrative transfer prices are usually based on cost, but may also be based on equity considerations designed around some definition of a reasonable division of a jointly earned revenue or a jointly incurred cost.

Responsibility Centers and Financial Control 191

Exhibit 12-21 summarizes advantages and disadvantages of the four major transfer-pricing approaches.

VII. Assigning and Valuing Assets in Investment Centers

    A. Using investment centers to evaluate responsibility center performance brings the problems associated with profit centers, plus additional problems:

        1. *Identifying assets* used by the investment center. Issues include how to assign responsibility for jointly used assets, such as cash and buildings and equipment, and for jointly created assets, such as accounts receivable.

        2. *Valuing assets* used by the investment center. A method of costing, such as historical cost or replacement cost, must be chosen.

Learning Objective 7: Use return on investment and economic value added as financial control tools.

VIII. Return on Investment and Economic Value Added

    A. Efficiency and Productivity Elements of Return on Investment

        1. Chapter 1 discussed Dupont's development of the return-on-investment (ROI) concept, which is often broken down into two components, return and turnover:

$$\begin{aligned} \text{ROI} &= \text{Operating Income}/\text{Investment} \\ &= \frac{\text{Operating Income}}{\text{Sales}} \times \frac{\text{Sales}}{\text{Investment}} \\ &= \text{Return on sales} \times \text{Asset turnover} \\ &= \text{Efficiency} \times \text{Productivity} \end{aligned}$$

        2. **Efficiency** is a measure of an organization's ability to control costs at a given level of sales activity. As shown, in financial control, this is the ratio of earnings to sales (also called return on sales or sales margin).

        3. **Productivity** is a ratio of output to input. In financial control, as shown, this is the ratio of sales to investment.

 Exhibit 12-22 displays a summarized version of the Dupont ROI Control System. Note the increasingly more detailed subcomponents for the efficiency and productivity measures.

B. Assessing Organization Efficiency and Productivity Using Financial Control

1. Most accounting approaches to assessing efficiency stress comparing costs with some standard. For example, one can define *operations efficiency* as standard cost divided by actual cost. The benchmark operations efficiency measure is 100%, and an efficiency measure below 100% implies inefficient operations.

2. A widely accepted definition of productivity is the ratio of output over input. Organizations develop productivity measures for all factors of production, including people, raw materials, and equipment. For example, the ratio of raw material in the finished product to the total quantity of raw material acquired is called **raw material productivity** or **yield**.

C. Assessing Return on Investment: Ratio Trends

1. The return on investment approach requires a definition of what is meant by investment. The textbook example measures investment as total assets employed minus accumulated depreciation.

2. ROI can be computed and decomposed into its efficiency and productivity measures. These measures, as well as total ROI, are most useful when evaluating trends over time and when comparing the numbers with those of the best competitor.

   a. Trend (time series) analysis compares sequential measures for the same organization.

   b. Cross-sectional analysis compares the same measure for different organizations during the same time period.

3. This type of analysis can be very useful, but it is only a first step. *Ratio analysis does not identify a problem or a solution. Rather, it points to where analysis can begin.*

4. ROI should be viewed as a method to evaluate the desirability of long-term investments, rather than as a way to measure the short-term performance of a manager. A particularly undesirable situation arises when the manager is motivated to make return on investment as large as possible. In this case, the manager may inappropriately turn down projects whose internal rate of return exceeds the organization's cost of capital.

Study **Exhibits 12-23** through **12-27** on Dorchester Manufacturing for an illustration of the use of ratio trends.

D. Economic Value Added

1. **Economic value added** analysis (a form of residual income), equals income less the economic cost of the investment used to generate that income. That is, economic value added is the segment's income, less a financial charge that is computed by multiplying the cost of capital by the investment in the segment.

2. In one extension to *economic value added*, the income amount and the investment amount used to compute economic value added is GAAP income adjusted to reverse the conservative bias introduced by GAAP. For example, GAAP requires the immediate expensing of research and development costs, but in computing economic value added, research and development costs are capitalized and expensed over a number of years.

3. Economic value added is used to encourage managers to improve the relationship between return and assets employed. To evaluate possible improvements, managers can use activity-based costing to calculate economic value added by product, product line, or customer.

4. Unlike with ROI, a manager attempting to maximize economic value added should undertake investments that are expected to earn more than their cost of capital.

Learning Objective 8: Identify the limitations of financial controls.

IX. The Efficacy of Financial Control

A. Financial control may be an ineffective control scorecard for three reasons:

1. Measures of financial control are too narrow and do not measure other important performance variables, such as product or service quality and customer service.

2. Financial control measures the financial effect of the overall level of performance achieved on the critical success factors and ignores the performance achieved on the individual critical success factors. Effective control begins with measuring and managing the elements or processes that create financial returns.

3. Financial control usually focuses on short-term results. This is not a problem inherent to financial control. Rather, it is a problem relating to how financial control can be misused. A short-term focus can be debilitating for all employees, especially because this kind of an orientation produces behaviors that are not in the best long-run interests of the organization.

B. When used properly, financial control can provide crucial help in managing an organization. Financial control must be supported by other tools or perspectives, such as the balanced scorecard described in Chapter 10.

PRACTICE TEST QUESTIONS AND PROBLEMS

True/False

_____ 1. An unfavorable variance is one in which actual costs are less than estimated costs.

_____ 2. Material usage and price variances are examples of third-level variances.

_____ 3. Efficiency and wage rate variances pertain to direct labor costs.

_____ 4. Centralization is more suited (than is decentralization) to entities whose environments are stable.

_____ 5. To assess variances accurately when actual volume differs from planned volume, flexible budgets should be used.

_____ 6. Investment centers are a combination of profit and cost centers.

_____ 7. The controllability principle applies only to managers of cost centers.

_____ 8. If Division A supplies goods to Division B, and both divisions are investment centers, the transfer price will affect the incomes of both divisions.

_____ 9. When a good or service has no market price, one alternative is to use cost as a basis for a transfer price.

_____ 10. Cost-based transfer pricing provides incentives to the supplying division to control costs.

_____ 11. Another way to state ROI is Efficiency × Productivity.

_____ 12. ROI measures are most useful when evaluating trends over time and when comparing the numbers with those of the best competitor.

_____ 13. *Economic value added* is a variation of the ROI formula.

Multiple-Choice

1. The difference between first- and second-level variance analyses is
   (a) the level of disaggregation and detail of analysis.
   (b) that first-level applies to direct materials, while second-level applies to direct labor.
   (c) that second-level applies to direct materials, while first-level applies to direct labor.
   (d) that second-level analysis is less detailed than first-level.

2. Which of the formulae below correctly illustrates the calculation for the direct labor efficiency variance?
   (a) $(AR - SR) \times AH$
   (b) $(AR - SR) \times SH$
   (c) $(AH - SH) \times AR$
   (d) $(AH - SH) \times SR$

3. The formula for the total direct labor cost variance is
   (a) $(AR \times AH) - (SR \times SH)$.
   (b) $(SR \times AH) - (AR \times SH)$.
   (c) $(AR \times SR) - (SR \times SH)$.
   (d) $(AR \times SH) - (SR \times AH)$.

4. Given the following information, calculate the materials price variance for direct materials: $AP = \$250$; $SP = \$245$; $AQ = 20$.
   (a) $100F
   (b) $100U
   (c) $230U
   (d) $225U

5. Each of the following is true about centralization, EXCEPT
   (a) centralization is more suited to organizations in stable environments.
   (b) centralization is more suited to organizations in which technology and customer requirements are well understood.
   (c) centralization is more suited to organizations in which product lines are mostly of the commodity type.
   (d) under centralization, employee empowerment programs are firmly in place.

6. Investment center managers are responsible for
   (a) costs and investments.
   (b) revenues.
   (c) revenues and investments.
   (d) costs, revenues, and investments.

7. Segment margin reports should be interpreted carefully because
   (a) the segment margin may contain numbers that are quite arbitrary.
   (b) segment margins do not take variable costs into account.
   (c) segment margins do not take fixed costs into account.
   (d) segment margins are never calculated by product line.

8. Which of the following transfer-pricing methods are set by the application of a rule or policy?
   (a) Market-based transfer price
   (b) Administered transfer price
   (c) Cost-based transfer price
   (d) Negotiated transfer price

9. The biggest problem with market-based transfer prices is that
   (a) they do not allow both parties to calculate unit incomes.
   (b) they require too much negotiation.
   (c) market prices seldom exist.
   (d) they do not provide the proper economic guidance.

10. Return on investment is the ratio of
    (a) operating income to productivity.
    (b) efficiency to investment.
    (c) operating income to investment.
    (d) operating income to sales.

11. If ROI = 20%, the sales level is $1,000,000, and the investment level is $1,500,000, what is the operating income?
    (a) $7,500,000
    (b) $5,000,000
    (c) $ 300,000
    (d) $ 200,000

12. If, for purposes of computing economic value added, accounting income is 12% of sales, $3,000,000 of capital is used, the cost of capital is 9%, and sales is revenue is $15,000,000, what is the economic value added?
    (a) $1,530,000
    (b) $ 990,000
    (c) $ 900,000
    (d) $ 450,000

13. All of the following are true about cost center control, EXCEPT
    (a) cost centers should be evaluated solely on their ability to control costs.
    (b) interperiod cost comparisons can be misleading when the production mix or the production levels are changing.
    (c) flexible budgets should be used to compute variances from actual results.
    (d) when flexible budget costs are greater than actual costs, the variances are labeled "favorable."

14. Financial control is thought by some to be an ineffective method of control for all of the reasons below, EXCEPT
    (a) financial control often ignores nonquantitative factors such as quality and customer satisfaction.
    (b) financial control measures the overall effect of performance on critical success factors, but does not provide direct insight on individual critical success factors.
    (c) financial control is often oriented toward short-term performance.
    (d) financial control does not provide an overall assessment of whether the organization's strategies and decisions are providing acceptable financial returns.

Completion

1. Variance analysis is a set of procedures to help managers understand the source of differences between _____ and _____ costs.

2. The formula for calculating material usage variances is (AQ − ___) × ____.

3. Efficiency and wage rate variances are associated with _____ _____ _____.

4. _____ variances are the cost differences between the master budget and the flexible budget.

5. _____ _____ variances show the difference between the flexible budget and actual results.

6. _____ allows organization members to identify changing customer tastes quickly and gives employees authority and responsibility.

7. _____ control focuses on finding the best operating decisions; _____ control focuses on an overall assessment of how well systems are working to create financial results.

8. Cost centers are _____ centers whose employees control costs but do not control their _____ or _____ level.

9. Some _____ centers control the mix of stock carried, price, and promotional activities.

10. A _____ center is like an independent business except that senior management controls the level of investment.

11. A _____ _____ is the level of controllable profit reported by an organization unit or product line.

12. Numbers that can be quite arbitrary because they rest on subjective assumptions over which there can be legitimate disagreement are called _____ numbers.

13. If an organization is committed to the spirit of determining the income of each responsibility center, _____ _____ are the most appropriate basis for transferring goods or services between responsibility centers.

14. Some critics object to _____ _____ _____ because the resulting profits of the responsibility centers reflect both economic considerations and negotiating skills, rather than purely economic considerations.

15. Using investment centers to evaluate responsibility center performance brings the problems of _____ assets and _____ assets used by the investment center.

16. Return on investment = return on sales × _____ _____.

Problems

1. You have just purchased a fast-food franchise called Chicken Fixin's. Worldwide there are 700 such franchises. Do you think that your franchise can be run as an investment center?

2. Compare and contrast the four major methods of transfer prices: market-based transfer prices, cost-based transfer prices, negotiated transfer prices, and administered transfer prices.

3. Drane Company shows the following information for job M337:

Actual:		
	Direct materials used:	9000 lbs. purchased at $2.00 per lb.
	Direct labor:	1700 hours at $9.50 per hour
	Units produced:	600 units
Standard:		
	Direct materials:	18 lbs. per unit at $1.80 per lb.
	Direct labor:	3 hours per unit at wage rate of $9.00 per hour

(a) Determine the material price and use variances.

(b) Determine the direct labor wage rate and efficiency variances.

SOLUTIONS TO PRACTICE TEST QUESTIONS AND PROBLEMS

True/False

1. False. An unfavorable variance arises when actual costs are greater than estimated costs.

2. True. These are third-level variances for direct materials. A first-level variance for cost items is the difference between actual and master budget costs for that item. The planning variance and the flexible budget variance are second-level variances. Third-level variances decompose the flexible budget variances.

3. True. Efficiency and wage rate variances are calculated for direct labor costs.

4. True. Centralization is more suited to entities whose environments are stable.

5. True. Flexible budgets, which are projected costs given the volume and mix of activities undertaken, should be used when actual volume differs from planned volume.

6. False. Investment centers are responsibility centers whose managers control revenues, costs, and the level of investment.

7. False. The controllability principle applies to managers of all types of responsibility centers, which are simply organization units for which a manager has been made responsible.

8. True. The transfer price represents sales revenue for Division A and cost for Division B.

9. True. When a good or service has no market price, one alternative is to use cost as a basis for a transfer price. Cost-based transfer prices introduce a number of problems, however.

10. False. Cost-based transfer pricing does *not* provide incentives to the supplying division to control costs, because the supplier can always recover its costs.

11. True. Another way to state ROI is: Efficiency × Productivity, where Efficiency = Return on sales, and Productivity = Asset turnover.

12. True. Total ROI, as well as its associated submeasures, can be tracked using trend analysis or cross-sectional analysis

13. False. Economic value added relies on the residual income concept. That is, economic value added is a segment's income, minus the cost of capital multiplied by the investment in the segment.

Multiple-Choice

1. a. The difference between first- and second-level variance analysis is the level of disaggregation and detail of analysis. Second-level variances disaggregate first-level variances.

2. d. The correct formula is: $(AH - SH) \times SR$.

3. a. The correct formula is: $(AR \times AH) - (SR \times SH)$.

4. b. The materials price variance is $(AP - SP) \times AQ$ or $(\$250 - \$245) \times 20 = \$100\ U$, because actual usage was greater than the estimate.

5. d. In most centralized firms, decision making is centralized and employee empowerment programs are not overly abundant.

6. d. Investment center managers are responsible for costs, revenues, and investments.

7. a. Segment margins should be interpreted because they may contain numbers that are quite arbitrary. In addition, financial segment margin analysis should be supplemented by performance assessments on other critical success factors.

8. b. Administered transfer prices are set by the application of a rule or policy.

9. c. The biggest problem with market-based transfer prices is that market prices seldom exist.

10. c. Return on investment is the ratio of operating income to investment.

11. c. ROI = Operating income/Investment; 0.20 = Operating income/$1,500,000, so Operating income = $300,000. The sales level is unnecessary in solving this problem.

12. a. Economic value added = accounting income − cost of capital times investment; 12% ($15,000,000) − 9% ($3,000,000) = $1,530,000.

13. a. Cost centers should be also be evaluated on quality and other critical nonfinancial indicators.

14. d. Financial control does provide an overall assessment of whether the organization's strategies and decisions are providing acceptable financial returns.

Completion

1. estimated or budgeted, actual
2. *SQ, SP*
3. direct labor costs
4. Planning
5. Flexible budget
6. Decentralization
7. Operations, financial
8. responsibility, revenues, investment
9. revenue
10. profit
11. segment margin
12. soft
13. market prices
14. negotiated transfer prices
15. identifying, valuing
16. asset turnover

Problems

1. As manager of Chicken Fixin's, you will probably have very little control over the food that you will be serving, prices that you can charge, and the kind of advertising that you can use. This is because many of these decisions will be made at the corporate level. However, as manager, you can control the level and quality of customer service, personnel, and cleanliness. These are critical variables to maximize return business. In addition, the major aspects of an investment center, such as building costs and inventory, are not controllable by the manager. Thus, it is more appropriate to operate this type of business as a profit center.

2. Market-based prices have the advantage of being objective and provide the appropriate economic incentives as long as a market price exists. A key disadvantage is that no market prices may be available for the exact product transferred. Cost-based prices are relatively easy to use, as the data are usually available from the cost accounting system. There are many transfer-price variations associated with costs; any variation other than marginal cost will not provide the right economic incentives. Negotiated transfer prices do reflect the concept of responsibility, but because negotiating skill is a critical factor in determining prices, critics charge that such prices do not reflect enough of the economics of the situation. Finally, administered transfer prices are simple to administer, as they are based on established rules. However, administratively set prices violate the spirit that underlies the responsibility philosophy.

3. (a) Materials price variance = $(AP - SP) \times AQ = (\$2.00 - \$1.80) \times 9{,}000$
   = \$1,800 Unfavorable

   Materials quantity variance = $(AQ - SQ) \times SP = [9{,}000 - (18 \times 600)] \times \$1.80$
   = \$3,240 Favorable

   (b) Direct labor wage rate variance = $(AR - SR) \times AH = (\$9.50 - \$9.00) \times 1{,}700$
   = \$850 Unfavorable

   Direct labor efficiency variance = $(AH - SH) \times SR = [1{,}700 - (3 \times 600)] \times \$9$
   = \$900 Favorable